1/14

D0576152

Tobacco
Through the Smoke Screen

ILLICIT AND MISUSED DRUGS

Illicit and Misused Drugs

Tobacco
Through the Smoke Screen

by Zachary Chastain

Mason Crest

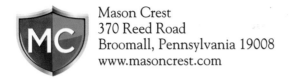

Mason Crest
370 Reed Road
Broomall, Pennsylvania 19008
www.masoncrest.com

Copyright © 2013 by Mason Crest, an imprint of National High-lights, Inc. All rights reserved. No part of this publication may be reproduced or transmitted in any form or by any means, electronic or mechanical, including photocopying, recording, taping, or any information storage and retrieval system, without permission from the publisher.

Printed in the Hashemite Kingdom of Jordan.

First printing
9 8 7 6 5 4 3 2 1

Library of Congress Cataloging-in-Publication Data

Chastain, Zachary.
Tobacco : through the smoke screen / Zachary Chastain.
    p. cm. — (Illicit and misused drugs)
Includes bibliographical references and index.
ISBN 978-1-4222-2442-7 (hardcover)
ISBN 978-1-4222-2461-8 (paperback)
ISBN 978-1-4222-2424-3 (series hardcover)
ISBN 978-1-4222-9306-5 (ebook)
  1. Tobacco use—Prevention—Juvenile literature. 2. Tobacco—History—Juvenile literature. 3. Smoking—Juvenile literature. I. Title.
  HV5735.C43 2012
  362.29'6—dc23
                                    2011032594

Interior design by Benjamin Stewart.
Cover design by Torque Advertisng + Design.
Produced by Harding House Publishing Services, Inc.
www.hardinghousepages.com

This book is meant to educate and should not be used as an alternative to ap-propriate medical care. Its creators have made every effort to ensure that the information presented is accurate—but it is not intended to substitute for the help and services of trained professionals.

 # CONTENTS

INTRODUCTION

Addicting drugs are among the greatest challenges to health, well-being, and the sense of independence and freedom for which we all strive—and yet these drugs are present in the everyday lives of most people. Almost every home has alcohol or tobacco waiting to be used, and has medicine cabinets stocked with possibly outdated but still potentially deadly drugs. Almost everyone has a friend or loved one with an addiction-related problem. Almost everyone seems to have a solution neatly summarized by word or phrase: medicalization, legalization, criminalization, war-on-drugs.

For better and for worse, drug information seems to be everywhere, but what information sources can you trust? How do you separate misinformation (whether deliberate or born of ignorance and prejudice) from the facts? Are prescription drugs safer than "street" drugs? Is occasional drug use really harmful? Is cigarette smoking more addictive than heroin? Is marijuana safer than alcohol? Are the harms caused by drug use limited to the users? Can some people become addicted following just a few exposures? Is treatment or counseling just for those with serious addiction problems?

These are just a few of the many questions addressed in this series. It is an empowering series because it provides the information and perspectives that can help people come to their own opinions and find answers to the challenges posed by drugs in their own lives. The series also provides further resources for information and assistance, recognizing that no single source has all the answers. It should be of interest and relevance to areas of study spanning biology, chemistry, history, health, social studies and more. Its efforts to provide a real-world context for the information that is clearly presented but not overly simplified should be appreciated by students, teachers, and parents.

The series is especially commendable in that it does not pretend to pose easy answers or imply that all decisions can be made on the basis of simple facts: some challenges have no immediate or simple solutions, and some solutions will need to rely as much upon basic values as basic facts. Despite this, the series should help to at least provide a foundation of knowledge. In the end, it may help as much by pointing out where the solutions are not simple, obvious, or known to work. In fact, at many points, the reader is challenged to think for him- or herself by being asked what his or her opinion is.

A core concept of the series is to recognize that we will never have all the facts, and many of the decisions will never be easy. Hopefully, however, armed with information, perspective, and resources, readers will be better prepared for taking on the challenges posed by addictive drugs in everyday life.

— *Jack E. Henningfield, Ph.D.*

1 What Is Tobacco?

Tobacco is a tall plant with broad leaves, native to North and South America. Tobacco (genus *Nicotiana*) belongs to the *solanaceae* or nightshade family, which includes other shrubs, trees, weeds, and crop plants (such as potatoes). Tobacco is a resilient plant known to grow in many different soils and climates. In fact, over fifty different species of tobacco grow all over the world. For the purposes of this book, however, we'll focus on only two of those species: *Nicotiana tabacum*, **indigenous** to South America, and *Nicotiana rustica*, indigenous to North America along the Mississippi River and lower Eastern Canada. Today, *Nicotiana tabacum* is the species most widely cultivated for cigarette use because its leaves produce mild smoke.

What Does Tobacco Look Like Today?

The Cigarette

Most tobacco today is packaged in the form of a cigarette. More than ever, young people are at risk for nicotine addiction through cigarettes. Many kids believe they can smoke for a few years and then quit. Unfortunately, this is rarely true. Smokers who start young fall into three categories: those who immediately become addicted, those who gradually become addicted, and those who smoke lightly and never become addicted. Cigarette companies would like us to believe the last category is always true, but in reality it rarely is. Cigarettes are designed to addict: they are chemically engineered to deliver nicotine to your brain.

Cigarettes are designed to cause addiction.

Did You Know?

Tobacco smoke contains more than four thousand chemicals, most of them dangerous to your health.

Chemicals in tobacco:	as found in:
acetone	paint stripper
ammonia	floor cleaner
arsenic	ant poison
butane	lighter fluid
cadmium	car batteries
carbon monoxide	car exhaust fumes
DDT	insecticides
hydrogen cyanide	gas chambers
methanol	rocket fuel
naphthalene	mothballs
toluene	industrial solvent
vinyl chloride	plastics

Cigarette smoke contains many dangerous chemicals—from acetone (found in paint stripper) to carbon monoxide (found in car exhaust fumes.) Cigarette smoke also contains *toxic* gases, including carbon monoxide, hydrogen cyanide, and formaldehyde. Nicotine is the natural chemical in tobacco that makes smoking addictive, and unnatural chemicals added to tobacco make a cigarette deadly. These chemicals are given the general name "tar," and include everything in a cigarette but nicotine and water. These compounds comprise a cigarette's lethal "delivery system," designed to efficiently send high doses of nicotine to the brain. Tar infiltrates your lungs, and nicotine "rides" tar into the bloodstream. Over four thousand compounds are present in cigarette smoke to make the "rush" of nicotine faster and more enjoyable.

FAST FACT

Eighty-four percent of Canadian adults who smoke begin before they reach age twenty.

At least sixty of these chemical compounds are known or suspected to be carcinogens (cancer-forming chemicals).

Many people are under the false impression cigarettes are the only dangerous source of tobacco. They believe other tobacco products offer less dangerous nicotine delivery. But this is not true.

Cigars

Cigars are basically compact tobacco leaves rolled and prepared for smoking. The tobacco leaves in cigars are usually aged for a year, then fermented for three to five months. Cigars were traditionally considered "upscale" smokes, chosen by older wealthy smokers only, but recent studies have shown cigar smoking to be popular among teens and even preteens.

Many people think cigars are safe compared to cigarettes but that misperception has more to do with the habits of past generations of cigar smokers than the cigar itself. In the past, cigar smokers tended to start later in age than cigarette smokers and many cigar smokers did not regularly inhale the smoke, in part because of the more irritating nature of the smoke and in part because the nicotine could be more effectively absorbed without inhalation. This meant that cigars were responsible for less incidents of lung disease than cigarettes. But with the explosion of cigar use in the 1990s, people began smoking younger, smoking both cigars and cigarettes, and inhaling more. Adding to the risks, some cigars can deliver as much tar and nicotine as a pack or more of cigarettes, exposing their users and nearby nonusers to very high levels of disease-causing poisons.

Another myth is that expensive hand-rolled cigars do not have the deadly chemicals as cigarettes. In fact, their smoke is every bit as poisonous, and they can contain many of the same pesticide residues and other chemicals as cigarettes. Even the most "natural" cigar can put you at risk for health problems.

FAST FACT

Twenty percent of both American and Canadian deaths can be attributed to smoking.

Smokeless Tobacco

Smokeless tobacco is another dangerous substance. Snuff, chewing tobacco, and gutka are three popular forms of smokeless tobacco.

Snuff was once popular in England, where it was a fine powder snorted into the nose, but today it is a rough tobacco powder tucked between the lower lip and gum, where nicotine absorbs into the bloodstream.

Chewing tobacco (or simply "chew") is sold as leaf tobacco, packed in a pouch, or as plug tobacco, sold in brick form. In both forms, chewing tobacco is stuffed between the gum and cheek.

Gutka is a mix of lime paste, areca nut, spices, and tobacco sealed inside plastic or foil. Gutka is popular mainly in India and other Asian countries. In India, Gutka is more socially acceptable than smoking, and responsible for almost 75,000 to 80,000 new cases of oral cancer in India every year. Sadly, many children use gutka because it tastes like candy and has the texture of chewing gum.

Flavored Cigarettes

Bidis (pronounced *beedies*) are another tobacco product popular in India. They are small handmade, flavored cigarettes tied with colorful threads at each end. Teens in India (and increasingly in the United States and Canada) are finding bidis attractive because of their color and flavor and the misconception that they are safer than conventional cigarettes. Nothing could be farther from the truth. Smokers often get more cancer-causing chemicals from bidis than from conventional cigarettes. Bidis are wrapped in tendu leaves, native to India, and are much less porous than the paper wrapping of American cigarettes, making bidis' smoke more concentrated and dangerous.

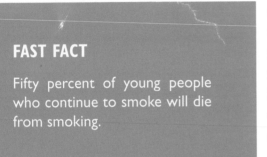

FAST FACT

Fifty percent of young people who continue to smoke will die from smoking.

Kreteks (clove cigarettes) are smoked by about 90 percent of Indonesian smokers, and are also popular in surrounding countries and especially in China. Cloves are gaining popularity in the United States and Canada as well. They look much like an American cigarette, but they contain a blend of herbs and fruit extracts. Some people replace normal cigarettes with cloves in an attempt to reduce health risks, but cloves are no safer.

Hookahs

The hookah often escapes scrutiny because of its relaxed, social nature. A hookah is a large water pipe with a slender hose for inhalation. Hookahs have become popular in cafés and lounge bars near colleges and universities,

The History of Hookahs
(according to the World Health Organization)

Waterpipes have been used to smoke tobacco and other substances by the indigenous peoples of Africa and Asia for at least four centuries. According to one historical account, a waterpipe was invented in India by a physician during the reign of Emperor Akbar (who ruled from 1556 to 1605) as a purportedly less harmful method of tobacco use. The physician Hakim Abul Fath suggested that tobacco smoke should be first passed through a small receptacle of water so that it would be rendered harmless. Thus, a widespread but unsubstantiated belief held by many waterpipe users today that the practice is relatively safe is as old as the waterpipe itself. Marketing tools associated with waterpipes and waterpipe tobacco may reinforce this unsubstantiated belief. For example, the label of a popular waterpipe tobacco brand sold in South-West Asia and North America states, "0.5% nicotine and 0% tar."

or in neighborhoods where many Yemeni, Moroccans, Egyptians, and other Arab immigrants live. According to Danny McGoldrick, research director for the Campaign for Tobacco-Free Kids, hookah-smoke is still addictive and dangerous, though it tastes sweet in the mouth and cool when inhaled.

Understanding Tobacco

This book will equip you with the facts: what tobacco is, where it came from, how our society has adopted it, how it can harm you, and what

FAST FACT

In the United States, the average age for a first cigarette is thirteen.

Health Effects of Hookahs
(According to the World Health Organization)

Contrary to ancient lore and popular belief, the smoke that emerges from a waterpipe contains numerous toxins known to cause lung cancer, heart disease, and other diseases. Waterpipe tobacco smoking delivers the addictive drug nicotine and, as is the case with other tobacco products, more frequent use is associated with the smokers being more likely to report that they are addicted. A waterpipe smoking session may expose the smoker to more smoke over a longer period of time than occurs when smoking a cigarette. Cigarette smokers typically take eight to twelve 40–75 milliter puffs over about 5 to 7 minutes and inhale 0.5 to 0.6 liters of smoke. In contrast, waterpipe smoking sessions typically last 20–80 minutes, during which the smoker may take 50 to 200 puffs, which range from about 0.15 to 1 liter each. The waterpipe smoker may therefore inhale as much smoke during one session as a cigarette smoker would inhale consuming 100 or more cigarettes. This puts waterpipe smokers at risk for the same kinds of diseases as are caused by cigarette smoking, including cancer, heart disease, respiratory disease, and adverse effects during pregnancy.

Tobacco Use Shortens Your Life

According to the Palo Alto Medical Foundation, every cigarette you smoke takes away seven minutes of your life. On average, it's estimated that someone who smokes a pack or more of cigarettes each day lives seven years less that someone who never smoked. The U.S. Centers for Disease Control and Prevention (CDC) estimates that annually in the United States, premature deaths from smoking related conditions collectively rob those who have died of nearly *five million years* from what would have been their normal life spans had they not smoked. And if current trends continue, the CDC projects that five million young people (under age eighteen) who are alive today will die prematurely as adults because they chose to start smoking as adolescents.

The Pollution of Secondhand Smoke

According to the CDC, secondhand smoke...

- fills the air with many of the same poisons found over toxic waste dumps.
- irritates eyes the way other pollutants do (redness, watering, itching).
- causes thirty times as many lung cancer deaths as other air pollutants.
- (in a crowded restaurant) can produce six times the pollution of a busy highway.
- causes 300,000 lung infections in infants and young children each year.
- kills three thousand nonsmokers each year from lung cancer alone.

you can do to end addiction. It is more important than ever to have correct information about tobacco during a time when cigarette companies and popular culture have made tobacco seem "cool" and appealing.

Unlike cocaine, heroin, or other dangerous drugs, tobacco's poison can go undetected for many years. Tobacco can gradually create addiction, and gradually kill. Tobacco is legal and accessible, but it is one of the leading causes of death throughout the world, causing almost half-a-million deaths in the United States annually.

You have the choice to be a statistic—80 to 90 percent of adult smokers began smoking before they were eighteen—or to be part of the change. Decide for yourself.

RIAPEIA VEL NICOTIANA
MAS MINOR

Schwant Kraut oder Tab
Mennlin das Klainer.

2 The History of Tobacco

For centuries, tobacco has played a large role in many cultures. This addictive plant has a long history, one that has changed through the years.

Native Americans and Tobacco

For Native Americans, tobacco was a medicine, sacred plant, and valuable trading *currency*. Historians believe that tobacco began growing in the Americas as early as 6000 BCE—long before Christopher Columbus and his men ever stepped foot on American soil. Over many years, natives in Central America developed various methods of tobacco consumption. The Mayans were likely the first people to spread the practice of tobacco smoking throughout North America. When they scattered north toward the Mississippi Valley, they brought their pipes and smoking ceremonies with them. Some

Gerry Rainingbird, a Native American, speaks about early tobacco use:

"The original purpose of [smoking tobacco] was to keep away the pests because tobacco has nicotine, which is a natural pesticide. But then it also evolved into this idea: it will also keep away the spirits that want to harm us as well. Using it as a way to cleanse our beings, our spirits."

(Source: www.pbs.org)

Natives smoked tobacco in pipes during ceremonial meals; others rolled the leaves into simple cigars. Some southern tribes adopted tobacco into their own religions, believing their god, the almighty Manitou, would make himself visible in the rising smoke of tobacco leaves.

In their book *Southern Indian Myths and Legends*, Virginia Brown and Laurella Owens make it clear that for early Native Americans, tobacco was not a personal habit; it was used only for special occasions as a community ceremony. Early Natives believed tobacco had **mystical** powers, that its smoke warded off evil spirits and brought forth friendly ones.

The Creek placed such value on tobacco that they thought of it as a warrior and gave it the war name *hitci*. The Cherokee called tobacco *tsalu*, "fire in the mouth." In these native cultures, tobacco was so precious among tribes that it became a currency both sacred and valuable.

Tobacco Arrives in Europe

When Columbus encountered Natives in 1492, he did not understand why they regarded tobacco so highly.

Native Americans believed tobacco was a sacred plant with spiritual powers.

Native Americans and Tobacco Today

Many American Indians still consider tobacco to be a sacred plant essential to their religious practices. Some Native elders say that tobacco is used to connect the worlds Earth and Spirit, since the plant's roots go deep into the soil and its smoke rises high into the sky. Giving gifts of tobacco is an honored tradition for Native Americans: to offer someone tobacco is to ask that you and the person receiving the tobacco be of one heart, one mind, and one spirit.

Native writer Marie Aqiiaqwak, in the *Red Road Collective Newsletter*, writes:

> When we put sacred tobacco into our Sacred Pipes, we are also using that tobacco as a communicator to the sky world where all of our ancestors have gone on before us. We do not inhale the sacred smoke that comes from the pipe. When the smoke rises, it is taking our prayers with it up to the Creator and all of our relatives who have gone on before us. Our elders show us that when we finish with prayers, we sprinkle a small amount of tobacco on the drum. This is a way of giving back to and thanking the Creator for all he has given to us. Tobacco can be used on a daily basis as each new day is greeted with prayers of thankfulness. Many elders say to hold it in your prayers of thankfulness. They also add that you are to hold it in your left hand as this is the hand closer to your heart.

He and his men received tobacco from the Natives as a gift when they first arrived in the Caribbean. Columbus wrote, "The natives brought fruit, wooden spears, and certain dried leaves which gave off a distinct fragrance." Later, back onboard their ship, Columbus and his crew ate the fruit quickly but threw away the useless "dried leaves." They did not understand the significance of the Native Americans' gift. It would take another set of men, Rodrigo de Jerez and Luis de Torres, to adopt smoking and bring tobacco to European shores.

First European Smoker

Jerez and Torres were Spanish explorers in Cuba, and are usually credited as the first Europeans to document tobacco smoking. In their journals, Jerez and Torres recount Natives wrapping tobacco in other plant leaves, making what looked to Jerez like "a musket formed of paper." The journal goes on to tell how one end was lit and the smoke "drank" through the other end. Jerez and Torres did not understand completely, but Jerez was sufficiently intrigued, for he eventually became a smoker himself and brought his new habit back to Spain.

At home, Jerez's neighbors and friends were not as enthusiastic about tobacco. In fact, they were so frightened

Christopher Columbus was one of the first Europeans to encounter the many wonders of the New World—including tobacco.

by the smoke pouring out of his mouth and nose that they informed the authorities Jerez was practicing "devilry." Spanish **Inquisitors** imprisoned Jerez for seven years. During those years, however, many ships went back and forth between Europe and the "New World," and when Jerez was released, he found Europe in a craze for tobacco.

Tobacco: The Cash Crop

Europe's curiosity was piqued, and demand for tobacco was increasing, but it would still be many years before every European had a pouch of tobacco in their pocket. The seas of change take years to cross.

Men like Christopher Columbus, Amerigo Vespucci, and Rodrigo de Jerez undertook their long voyages because they believed in the New World's promise of wealth, power, and influence. In those days, captains

In the seventeenth century, tobacco became an important crop in the James-town colony.

Some early cultures had volatile reactions to tobacco. Here are a few historical rejections:

Acceptance of tobacco use was less than unanimous. In 1628, Shah Sefi punished two merchants for selling tobacco by pouring hot lead down their throats. In 1634, Czar Alexis of Russia created new penalties for smoking. For the first offense, the punishment was whipping, a slit nose, and transportation to Siberia. The punishment for the second offense was execution. A Chinese regulation of 1634 made the use or distribution of tobacco punishable by decapitation.

(Source: www.intheknowzone.com)

were given ships and crews and sent to the Americas to find vast treasures or even mythical "fountains of youth." Before long, tobacco became a similar treasure, its leaves representing not just a strange Native American gift—as it had appeared to Columbus—but rather golden fields of opportunity. Tobacco crops became a "cash crop" in the English colonies of America, where the leaf came to support an entire culture in the New World. In early mid-Atlantic colonies, tobacco was often used in place of money itself, becoming, literally, the New World's currency.

Opposition to Tobacco

Within fifty years, the Earth's shape changed from flat to round; maps continued to expand their perimeters; and many people included tobacco among an ever-changing world that was exhilarating—but dangerous if embraced too quickly. Initially, much of the nobility considered smoking a vulgar habit. Their prejudice was against the "savages" who introduced tobacco to Europeans on

American soil. King James I of England, in particular, spent much of his reign opposing tobacco, imposing hefty *importation* taxes. But tobacco proved to be an unstoppable force—even for a king.

Tobacco and Medicine

By 1511, smoking had become popular in Spain, and by 1531, tobacco was being cultivated in a Spanish colony, Santo Domingo. In fact, it seemed that everywhere a European ship planted its flag, a small tobacco crop sprang up beside it.

The increased demand was largely due to discovery of tobacco's medicinal qualities. Europeans thought it a "miracle drug" for an assortment of ailments. Gene Borrio notes in his www.tobacco.org timeline that tobacco was once believed to be an effective treatment for "**colic**, **nephritis**, **hysteria**, **hernia**, and **dysentery**, toothache, falling fingernails, worms, bad breath, lockjaw, and cancer, among other illnesses."

Not everyone in the medical community was convinced tobacco was a "miracle drug," however, and in

As early as four hundred years ago physicians (and their king) were aware of the tar found inside tobacco's many alkaloid compounds. Even as tobacco was being heralded as the greatest medicine of all time—"healing" everything from headaches to tumors—it was thought by some to be addictive and harmful to the body. King James I of England demonstrated his suspicions of tobacco's harmful qualities in 1605, when he wrote:

[Tobacco] makes a kitchen also oftentimes in the inward parts of men, soiling and infecting them with an unctuous and oily kind of Soote, as hath bene found in some great Tobacco takers, that after death were opened.

Native Americans smoked tobacco in peace pipes as part of official ceremonies between tribes or nations.

1602, a group of concerned doctors performed a study comparing tobacco smokers to **chimney sweeps**. The study found similarities in their illnesses: chimney sweeps suffered lung diseases caused by soot, and tobacco smokers had similar "soot" in their lungs. Today, we give this soot the general name "tar."

Despite early medical research, tobacco became increasingly popular. Before the twentieth century, the scientific link between tobacco and its health effects was still weak.

Cigars became popular in the United States when soldiers brought them home after the Mexican American War.

Evolution of Tobacco

Because of the Native American influence on early smoking, tobacco was mostly smoked by pipe in the seventeenth century. In the eighteenth century, however, popularity shifted from the pipe to snuff, especially in England, and in the mid- to late nineteenth century, cigars became the smoker's choice in England, the United States, and Canada. Cigars gained additional support in the United States, as smokers returning from the Mexican War brought home various Latin American cigars. In the southern United States, chewing tobacco continued to be the most popular form of tobacco.

Beginnings of the Tobacco Industry

The cigarette's origins are actually quite humble. Historians credit the Spanish poor with innovating this form of smoking when they began collecting stray tobacco from cigar-butts that had fallen into the street, and then rolling it into thin tubes of scrap paper. This is how cigarettes received their name, cigar-ette, which simply means "little cigar." Eventually, observant businessmen recognized that smokers' choices had broadened with the popularity of cigars, and saw the cigarette as the natural next step for tobacco.

In the mid-1800s, Philip Morris began selling his Turkish cigarettes in London, and in 1884, James Bonsack received the **patent** for the first cigarette-rolling machine. Once the tobacco industry had the tools for **mass production**, things moved quickly in the world of cigarettes.

The first victory for "Big Tobacco" came in 1906. That was the year the Federal Food and Drugs Act required all companies to label their food and drug prod-

*In 1875, R. J. Reynolds founded the company that manufactures Camel ciga-
rettes. Mr. Reynolds died in 1918 of cancer of the pancreas caused by chewing
tobacco.*

ucts with a list of contents. Tobacco companies were concerned nicotine would be a required listing. They argued in a court case that nicotine, because it was not used to cure any disease or illness, could not be considered a drug. They won the case, and nicotine was kept off cigarette packages.

World War I and II

World Wars I and II were the next steps toward addicting North Americans to cigarettes. During both wars, cigarettes were **rationed** to soldiers like food or ammunition, and military leaders praised cigarettes for the "calming" effect they had on soldiers in heavy battle situations. Large tobacco companies sent thousands of free, name-brand cigarettes to soldiers fighting overseas. With military leaders' support of smoking, not surprisingly, cigarette consumption increased dramatically during and after the wars. Tobacco even became a symbol of patriotism and the war effort against Germany. Entire generations of men and women were addicted to cigarettes through their shared war experience.

Women and Cigarettes

After World War I, smoking associated itself with another cause—women's rights. Before the war, many women looked down their nose on smoking as a dirty and disgusting habit, and few smoked. But as women pressed for the vote, the cigarette became more alluring. The cigarette represented an element of risk, a choice that proved women were not helpless or frightened of change. The cigarette was a small freedom, but many women began to see it as a symbol for greater freedom.

The cigarette was a fashion symbol as well. During the Roaring Twenties, a slim figure became more fashionable

When stars like Humphrey Bogart were portrayed smoking, it helped make the connection in many Americans' minds between cigarettes, glamour, and sophistication.

than it had been in previous decades, and many women found cigarettes to be helpful appetite suppressors. Smoking's benefits were twofold: a woman could establish herself as self-sufficient and, at the same time, control her weight. Cigarette companies, of course, were more than happy to supply the cigarettes to keep women thin. Magazine advertisements for Lucky Strike cigarettes urged women to "Reach for a Lucky Instead of a Sweet."

The Glamour of Smoking

Cigarettes continued to integrate themselves into North America and abroad. Famous people of all sorts began smoking. In 1932, Americans elected the first president who was widely known to be a smoker, Franklin Delano Roosevelt. American baseball slugger Babe Ruth was a famous cigar smoker. Cigarettes were popular among artists, entertainers, and athletes; writers Ernest Hemingway, Isak Dinesen, and Albert Camus were all smokers, as were movie stars Clark Gable, Humphrey Bogart, and Bette Davis. Cigarette companies paid celebrities to endorse their products on increasingly popular radio programs. Advertising became one of Big Tobacco's most deadly weapons.

Cigarette companies marketed their product to children as early as 1890, when baseball cards were included with each pack of cigarettes, a precursor of the baseball card-chewing gum combination that would come later. But in the twentieth century, cigarette companies focused their attention on kids more than ever, using cartoon characters, free T-shirts, and prizes to lure younger smokers. Advertising often focused on the flavor and image of cigarettes, and downplayed the health effects.

Government Intervention

Government regulation of Big Tobacco in the United States started in 1965, when Congress required a rather weak caution label on each cigarette pack. In 1967, a Surgeon General's Report found smoking to be the principal cause of lung cancer, and also found evidence linking smoking to heart disease. In 1969 and 1970, Congress strengthened the cigarette labeling law, changing it to read, "Warning: the Surgeon General has Determined that Cigarette Smoking is Dangerous to Your Health." In those same years, President Nixon signed a law banning cigarette advertising on radio and television.

These laws proved to be too lax, however, and instead of limiting tobacco companies, they often gave them protection from further public attack. One law in particular said no additional notice could be placed on properly labeled cigarettes, meaning tobacco companies were free to sell their health-damaging product as long as they labeled it accordingly.

Contradictions like this have continued throughout the years; after all, the tobacco industry is an enormous economic and political force, and it won't be overthrown without a fight. The government created the Office on Smoking and Health (OSH) in 1980, and since then the organization has spent more than $20 million of taxpayers' money to educate the public on the dangers of smoking. Another organization, the U.S. Department of Agriculture (USDA), has spent more than $15 million to counteract tobacco's effects.

It seems strange that the government would condemn smoking and then spend so much money to support its existence, but perhaps it isn't so strange if one considers the amount of money that Big Tobacco invests in

C. Everett Koop became famous as the Surgeon General who officially declared that smoking is hazardous to your health.

Although cigars are sometimes considered to be safer than cigarettes, they can also cause cancer.

political campaigns. "They're giving such large amounts of money [to political campaigns], it's hard to believe they don't want something in return," says Representative Henry Waxman, a democrat from California.

Public Confrontation

Throughout the 1990s, a series of charges were brought against tobacco companies. Citizens harmed by tobacco made significant gains inside and outside the courtroom. In 1999, for example, the Phillip Morris tobacco company acknowledged:

> There is an overwhelming medical and scientific *consensus* that cigarette smoking causes lung cancer, heart disease, *emphysema* and other serious diseases in smokers . . . there is no safe cigarette . . . cigarette smoking is addictive, as that term is most commonly used today.

In addition to statements like this, some cigarette companies have also agreed to spend sums of money on nicotine-addiction research and antismoking programs for youth. Even so, in many places around the world there are no laws that limit or prohibit the sale of tobacco. In some countries, like China, tobacco is almost completely unregulated, and it is predicted that one-third of Chinese adults now under age twenty-nine will die of tobacco-related causes.

Clearly there is still much to be done—in North America and the world at large—before nicotine addiction is confronted on a larger scale.

Cigarette Package Warnings in the United States

1966 through 1970:
"CAUTION: CIGARETTE SMOKING MAY BE HAZARDOUS TO YOUR HEALTH"

1970 through 1985:
"WARNING: THE SURGEON GENERAL HAS DETERMINED THAT CIGARETTE SMOKING IS DANGEROUS TO YOUR HEALTH."

Since 1985 these four warnings have had to appear on cigarette packages (rotating quarterly):
"SURGEON GENERAL'S WARNING: Smoking Causes Lung Cancer, Heart Disease, Emphysema, and May Complicate Pregnancy."
"SURGEON GENERAL'S WARNING: Quitting Smoking Now Greatly Reduces Serious Risks to Your Health."
"SURGEON GENERAL'S WARNING: Smoking by Pregnant Women May Result in Fetal Injury, Premature Birth and Low Birth Weight."
"SURGEON GENERAL'S WARNING: Cigarette Smoke Contains Carbon Monoxide."

Cigarette Package Warnings in Canada

Sixteen different health-warning messages appear on Canadian tobacco product packages. Some of these messages include graphic photographs of oral cancer, diseased lungs, and in-your-face statements including:

"Tobacco products are highly addictive."
"Your chances of surviving [lung cancer] are low. Eighty percent of lung cancer victims die within one year."
"Tobacco use triples the risk of heart disease."
"Smoking during pregnancy can harm your baby."

Smokeless Tobacco Product Package Warnings in the United States

"WARNING: This product may cause mouth cancer."
"WARNING: This product may cause gum disease and tooth loss."
"WARNING: This product is not a safe alternative to cigarettes."

Cigar Package Warnings in the United States

"SURGEON GENERAL'S WARNING: Cigar Smoking Can Cause Cancers Of The Mouth And Throat, Even If You Do Not Inhale."
"SURGEON GENERAL'S WARNING: Cigar Smoking Can Cause Lung Cancer and Heart Disease."
"SURGEON GENERAL'S WARNING: Tobacco Use Increases The Risk of Infertility, Stillbirth And Low Birth Weight."
"SURGEON GENERAL'S WARNING: Cigars Are Not A Safe Alternative To Cigarettes."
"SURGEON GENERAL'S WARNING: Tobacco Smoke Increases The Risk Of Lung Cancer And Heart Disease, Even In Nonsmokers."

Warnings on Other Tobacco Product Labels in Canada

Bidis:

"USE OF THIS PRODUCT CAN CAUSE CANCER"
"TOBACCO SMOKE HURTS CHILDREN"
"TOBACCO SMOKE CAN CAUSE FATAL LUNG DISEASES"
"TOBACCO SMOKE CONTAINS HYDROGEN CYANIDE"

Chewing tobacco and oral snuff:

"THIS PRODUCT IS HIGHLY ADDICTIVE"
"THIS PRODUCT CAUSES MOUTH DISEASES"
"THIS PRODUCT IS NOT A SAFE ALTERNATIVE TO CIGARETTES"
"USE OF THIS PRODUCT CAN CAUSE CANCER"

Nasal snuff:

"THIS PRODUCT IS NOT A SAFE ALTERNATIVE TO CIGARETTES"
"THIS PRODUCT CONTAINS CANCER CAUSING AGENTS"
"THIS PRODUCT MAY BE ADDICTIVE"
"THIS PRODUCT MAY BE HARMFUL"

Warning on Cigarette Package Labels in France

"SMOKING KILLS."

3 Tobacco and Culture

Kenneth Warner, Ph.D., estimates the tobacco industry needs to recruit five thousand new young smokers every day to compensate for the thousands who die of tobacco-related illnesses every year. So, how do cigarette companies continue to sell a tobacco product that science has firmly linked to disease and illness? Where do cigarette companies continue to find their new customers? The answers, of course, are in the cultural history of cigarettes. The story is a long one.

A Brief History of Advertising

Just how images and banners affect the brain is a topic of much discussion today. The exact science of advertising is elusive. Scholars are beginning to research Americans, in particular, in order to understand susceptibility to advertising. Some believe Americans may be **genetically predisposed** to respond to advertising. Their research is based on historical evidence that the first large-scale advertising campaign in England was America itself.

America, or the "New World," was promoted as advertisers today might sell a new car or an exotic vacation package. Thousands of Europeans were enticed by the promises of land developers, salesmen, and relatives already in America. Today, America is comprised of people who emigrated from all over the world, from many different generations, and the story of advertising is one of financial success across many cultures.

Early cigarette advertising appealed to customers through America's first and best-loved sport—baseball. Each pack of cigarettes was sold with a baseball card, with the intention of creating associations between a favorite American pastime and cigarette smoking. The same basic principle of association continues to be used to this day. The formula for selling cigarettes remains the same; only the methods change.

As mentioned in chapter 2, World Wars I and II were extremely important in the war on smokers' lungs. Just as soldiers overseas were supplied with free cigarettes, Americans at home experienced the first large-scale marketing of cigarettes. Advertisements showed soldiers smoking cigarettes, guns slung over their shoulders, silhouettes against the setting sun. Cigarette companies associated their products with a positive message: support the war and be a patriot by smoking cigarettes.

Selling cigarettes to women required a different message. Tobacco companies responded in the 1920s by promoting cigarettes as "torches of freedom" for the women's rights movement, capitalizing on the traditionally male association with cigarettes. They advertised tobacco as a bridge from feminine to masculine, a way women could assume rights and freedoms traditionally reserved for

FALSE ADVERTISING

Camels, 1930s:

"Athletes say, 'Camels don't get your wind!'"

"So mild! You can smoke all you want!"

Juleps, 1940s:

"New miracle mint in Juleps freshens the mouth at every puff. Even if you chain-smoke, your mouth feels clean, sparkling all day long!"

Philip Morris, 1956:

"More vintage tobacco makes PHILIP MORRIS so popular with younger smokers."

men. Throughout the twentieth century, smoking continued to be marketed as an *emancipating* habit that was also romantic, sexually attractive, and sophisticated.

A single word—"slim"—has been extremely effective in selling cigarettes to women. In a society that places emphasis on women's physical attractiveness and a thin figure, cigarette companies had little work to do. In the 1930s, cigarette ads showed beautiful Hollywood stars like Rita Hayworth, Rosalind Russell, and Betty Grable smoking cigarettes that were long and thin, the same as the then-popular ideal feminine shape.

By the time the government banned cigarette ads from television and radio in 1971, millions of Americans were smokers. By then, almost every American could name a favorite movie, television, or radio star who smoked. Some celebrities, like Edward R. Murrow and Arthur Godfrey, starred in programs in which a cigarette never

Secondhand Smoke

Smoking is a practice that also affects the health of those around you. When you smoke, you don't just inhale all the toxins discussed earlier in this book; you exhale them into the air around you. Not only do you exhale these poisons, but the smoke released from a lit cigarette contains toxins as well. This poisonous discharge is called secondhand smoke, and secondhand smoke kills. When a nonsmoker inhales smoke from your cigarette, she inhales the same poisons you inhale when you smoke, which puts her at risk for the very same diseases you risk contracting. The CDC estimates that exposure to secondhand smoke causes an estimated three thousand lung cancer deaths each year among *nonsmoking* American adults.

left their hands. The cultural influence of cigarettes was already significant by then, and cigarette companies' profits suffered little under the new advertising ban; they quickly shifted their attention from television and radio to magazines and billboards.

In 1998, tobacco advertisements were banned from billboards also, but ads continued to appear in magazines to which children had access. Tobacco companies now had limited options for advertising, and were willing to pay large sums of money for magazine ads. In many cases, magazines printed tobacco ads beside articles warning readers about harmful chemicals in foods and medicines, endorsing one deadly product while condemning another.

Tobacco companies also turned to sponsorship to replace billboard advertising. Watch a racing event sometime, and notice some drivers' helmets, pants, and jackets are all covered with a cigarette company's logo. In Canada, tobacco sponsorship is illegal, but in many countries—such as the United States—it is still allowed.

In 2001, Canada launched a massive federal tobacco regulation program, a five-year, $480 million plan that focused on prevention, helping smokers quit, and keeping Canadians safe from secondhand smoke. Every year, smoking-related diseases kill over 45,000 Canadians—more than murder, suicide, car accidents, and alcohol combined. The Canadian government is taking that statistic very seriously.

Virginia Slim cigarettes were marketed to appeal especially to women.

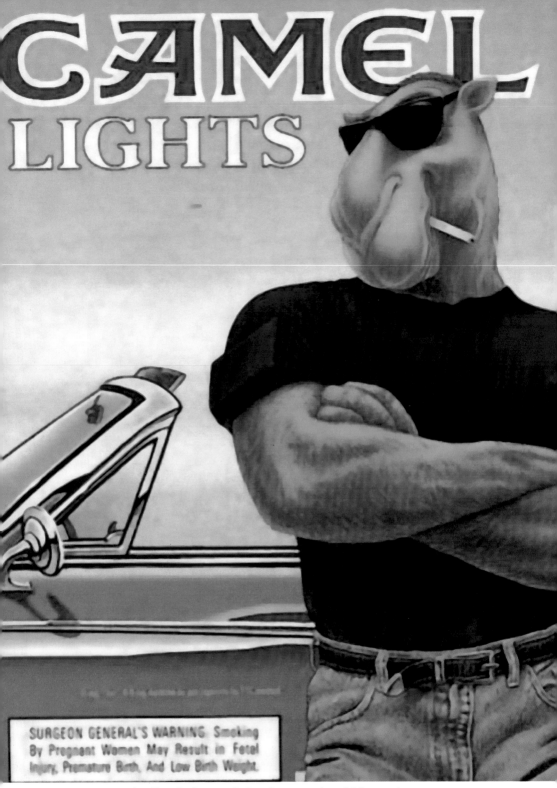

Joe Camel ads were designed to appeal to children and teens.

STRATEGIES CIGARETTE COMPANIES USE

Sponsorship: Sponsorship is prime advertising for tobacco companies. They simply sponsor events they want to associate with their products. Your favorite musician or tennis player might be sponsored by a cigarette company, but that doesn't mean cigarettes are musical or healthy.

Size: Tobacco promoters will make their products as big, wide, thin, or tall as possible. In their ads, they use tricks of scale to make cigarettes more appealing.

Retail promotion: Stores get paid by cigarette companies to exhibit counter-top displays and promotional posters for tobacco products and events. Smaller convenience stores are the primary target of tobacco companies, because they know young people are more likely to be there. A 1998 AC Nielson study, conducted for Health Canada, found that stores located close to schools and malls were more likely to carry counter-top displays and other promotions.

Product Placement: Cigarette ads can be almost anywhere, and tobacco companies are getting more creative. Even some video games, especially racing or driving games, will have players drive by virtual "billboards" advertising cigarettes.

Omission: This one is plain and simple: cigarette companies never show the ugly truth. You'll never see a haggard cancer patient, a young person with bronchitis coughing up phlegm, or someone with throat cancer. The truth gets left out of ads.

Individuality: Here is one strategy cigarette companies use frequently to attract young people. Don't buy it. Cigarettes can't make you an individual; only you can do that. One example of such ads is the Virginia Slims slogan: "Find your own voice."

Ideal People: Models in tobacco ads appear to be perfect. They're usually people with slim bodies, dressed fashionably to embody "cool" or "sexy." Women in tobacco ads tend to look sexy and alluring, while the men seem tough and masculine.

"Smoking Is a Good Time": Tobacco advertisers constantly send the message that everyone smokes, and everyone enjoys it. Images of happy smokers at parties, restaurants, and even in clean outdoor landscapes reinforce the connection between smoking and good times.

Facts and Figures: Tobacco advertisers have been known to use statistics and "pseudo-science" to give the impression that smoking is safe and to enhance their products' credibility.

Dreams and Insecurities: Tobacco advertisers use different strategies to attract males and females. Cigarette ads geared to young women play on the idea of being "liberated" and in control, while at the same time playing on insecurities about body image. Brands geared toward women often have words like "slim" or "slender" in the product name, or use extremely thin models in their ads. Cigarette ads targeting young men use rugged, independent, masculine-looking models, such as the classic image of the Marlboro Man. These models are usually shown participating in sports or outdoor activities, or surrounded by beautiful women.

Celebrity Smokers: Although tobacco companies can't use celebrity spokespeople in their ads, researchers have noted an increase in smoking by characters in movies, especially movies with teen appeal. Magazine photos of musicians, models, and actors smoking also promote the idea that smoking is glamorous.

The Cool Factor: By associating celebrities and "ideal" people with fun, excitement, and attitude, tobacco advertisers work hard to convince consumers that if they don't smoke, they're not cool. (There's even a brand of cigarette called "Kool"!)

(Source: Media Awareness Network)

Youth and Tobacco

Our world is becoming more visually oriented than ever before. The Internet provides today's youth with an easily accessible and vast source of information, one where they are bombarded by advertisements and images. Image processing and technology are easy and comfortable for today's young people. In fact, in many homes it isn't strange for a young girl or boy to teach their parents how to use the computer or digital camera. But experience with images makes today's youth more vulnerable to cigarette advertising than ever, and tobacco companies know this.

The 2009 National Survey on Drug Use and Health says that each day almost seven thousand people twelve or older try their first cigarette. The NSDUH also found that 58.8 percent of new cigarette smokers in 2009 were under age eighteen when they first smoked cigarettes. When all new smokers are taken into account, the average age of first cigarette use in 2009 was 17.4 years.

Studies done in the 1990s show that smoking among youth is increasing, not declining. Tobacco companies are determined to market their products to be attractive and "cool" to younger people. It's no coincidence that in 1994, the CDC reported 86 percent of underage smokers prefer Marlboro, Newport, or Camel—the three most heavily advertised brands of cigarettes.

Cigarettes and Minorities

Dave Goerlitz had been RJ Reynold's lead Winston cigarette model for seven years when he quit his job. In an interview with *The Times of London*, Goerlitz reported that when he quit, he asked an RJ Reynold's executive why a man who owned a tobacco company didn't smoke himself. The tobacco executive was disgusted: "We just sell it. We reserve the right to smoke for the young, the poor, the black and stupid."

Sadly, cigarette companies target smokers according to race, too. There is significant evidence showing cigarette companies have increasingly targeted minorities in the last decade. The first direct attack came in 1989, when RJ Reynolds began marketing its upcoming mentholated cigarette, "Uptown." Menthol was already very popular among African American smokers, and the introduction of Uptown cigarettes, packaged in a black and gold box, was a direct attack on African Americans. The cigarette ads for Uptown all featured young, healthy African Americans living exciting, wealthy lifestyles. RJ Reynolds even decided to release Uptown cigarettes in February of 1990, Black History Month, in order to take advantage of community activities and to distribute free cigarettes under "the radar." Fortunately, the black community struck back quickly, forming the multifaceted Coalition Against Uptown Cigarettes. Together, the coalition made RJ Reynolds' plans public and successfully defused Uptown cigarettes by January 1990.

Despite this victory, cigarettes continued to kill African Americans at higher rates than white smokers.

Published online at legacy.library.ucsf.edu, this excerpt is from a 1984 study by RJ Reynolds Tobacco:

"Since younger adult Blacks overwhelmingly prefer menthol cigarettes, continued emphasis on Salem within the Black market is recommended. Salem is already positioned against younger adults. With emphasis on the younger adult Black market, Salem may be able to provide an alternative to Newport and capitalize on Kool's decline."

Come to where the flavor is. Come to Marlboro Country

You get a lot to like with a Marlboro filter, flavor, pack or box.

Marlboro

Marlboro cigarette ads connected smoking with manliness and the American West.

ADVERTISING TO WOMEN

Virginia Slims: 1969
"You've come a long way, baby"

"In 1912, Lucille Watkins had to sneak out to the chicken coop to smoke a cigarette. You don't have to play hide and smoke anymore. Now there's even a cigarette for women only."

Virginia Slims: 1978
"You've come a long way, baby."

"Back then, every man gave his wife at least one day a week out of the house. You've come a long way, baby. Virginia Slims—Slimmer than the fat cigarettes men smoke."

Cigarette ads that appeal to women often make psychological connections between smoking, freedom, fun, and beauty.

Throughout the 1990s, researchers looked for explanation for the pattern, and found one in menthol. In 1998, the U.S. Surgeon General's Report on Tobacco Use in Racial/Ethnic Minorities suggested that menthol allows smokers to inhale more deeply, causing greater damage to the lungs. This may explain why African Americans smoke 35 percent fewer cigarettes per day than other smokers, yet still suffer higher death rates. Menthol cigarettes are deceptive: their name has associations with soothing cough drops, but their smoke is just as deadly.

Recently, there has been another outcrop of mentholated cigarettes marketed to minorities and, in particular, minority youth. Colorful images on boxes of Kool mentholated cigarettes depict the urban nightlife: disc jockeys, hip-hop clubs, young people captured dancing mid-air. Brands like "Kool Mixx" feature fruity flavors and are sometimes sold together with hip-hop CDs. Some cigarette companies have even begun sponsoring DJ competitions. The public has responded by accusing

The Light Option

"Low tar" and "low nicotine" cigarettes, also marketed as "light" or "ultra light" cigarettes, claim to have lower cancer risks. According to the CDC, however, cigarettes with lower tar and nicotine contents are not substantially less hazardous to your health than higher content brands. Smokers who switch to these brands often change their smoking habits—puffing more, inhaling more deeply, smoking more often—to make up for the reduced effects of less nicotine per cigarette, and end up consuming as many toxins, if not more, than had they stayed with regular brands.

"Smoking low tar and nicotine cigarettes is the equivalent of jumping out of the twenty-ninth floor of a building rather than the thirty-first."
—Kenneth Warner and John Slades in The American Journal of Public Health, January 1992

Cigarettes are marketed around the world, spreading tobacco's dangers to men, women, and children everywhere.

RJ Reynolds—producer of Kool Mixx, Kool Smooth Fusion, and Camel Exotic Blends—as well as Philip Morris—producer of Marlboro Menthol 72mm—of directly targeting youth with their "fruity" flavors and overtones of hip-hop culture.

In 2004, representatives from the health, African American, and Hispanic communities met in Atlanta to address these issues. According to the National Coalition of Hispanic Health, tobacco companies specifically target Hispanic, Latino, and African American consumers with advertising in low-income communities.

Women

The major theme of cigarette ads for women fifty years ago remains the same today: smoking is freedom, and smoking is slim. This first conceptualization of cigarettes—as "torches of freedom" for a new era—is extremely effective in the current age, as it cashes in on accomplishments of the woman's rights movement. Cigarettes' war on women has moved overseas with its message of false freedom. In developing and developed countries alike, tobacco companies are selling the idea that women need a cigarette to show their status as equals. One advertisement shows a young woman stating, "It's so me," and another ad emphasizes "The power of now." Some ads show women in high status, traditionally male occupations, such as airline pilots.

Cigarettes are being marketed to women using a variety of techniques. One is called "brand-stretching," advertising cigarette brand names on cashmere sweaters and designer jeans. In countries where direct cigarette advertising is illegal, tobacco products are promoted using a variety of products—from sunglasses, to purses, to bedding.

In countries like South Africa, cigarette ads go as far as using positive cultural values to sell their product. One ad showed a black woman accepting a cigarette from a white man, below the words, "Share the feeling, share the taste." Cigarette companies are smart. They adjust their strategies for each culture they hope to addict.

Meanwhile, tobacco's dangers put the entire world's health at risk.

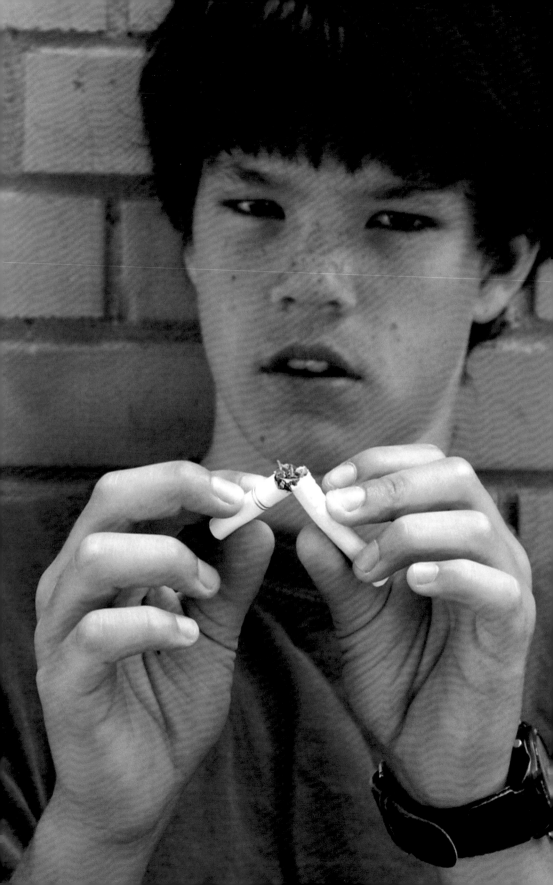

4 The Dangers of Tobacco

Tobacco has had an enormous impact on our culture. Its use affects entire nations' economy and health. Tobacco is deadly on the large scale—but it is equally deadly on the small scale, at the personal level.

How Smokers Get Started: Addiction

It begins with a substance called nicotine. Today, most people think of nicotine when they think of cigarettes—but that wasn't always the case. For decades, the majority of the public didn't believe cigarettes were addictive, and if they did, a strange substance called "nicotine" was unknown to them. Now the truth is out: nicotine is addictive.

A smoker's body doesn't adjust to nicotine; it develops a craving for it. Cigarette smokers gain increasing tolerance for nicotine, requiring more cigarettes and more smoke to satisfy their craving. Nicotine becomes a part of a smoker's body chemistry, and eventually—as is the case with heroin or cocaine addicts—the smoker's body doesn't feel normal anymore without nicotine in its system. And it doesn't stop there; cigarettes' addictive qualities may also result from a by-product of tobacco smoke called acetaldehyde. Research done on lab rats showed that rats were three times as addicted to nicotine when combined with acetaldehyde, a deadly combination found in every cigarette. This study was actually done by Philip Morris researchers, but the company shut down the laboratory and refused to let the researchers publish the findings until the FDA and the U.S. Congress made the findings public in the late 1990s.

Nicotine itself is an incredibly deadly chemical. Just two or three drops (50 milligrams) of pure nicotine on your tongue can kill you instantly. Nicotine is so deadly, in fact, that farmers and gardeners use it as an insecticide to protect crops.

This is how cigarettes deliver nicotine to your body: nicotine in cigarette smoke reaches your lungs' alveoli, where it rapidly absorbs into the bloodstream, often in as little as seven seconds, and the blood then carries it to the brain. The process is fast and extremely effective. In fact, smoked nicotine reaches the brain more quickly than heroin injected into the veins with a needle.

Establishing nicotine as an addictive substance was important in helping governments begin to properly educate the public, and it also gave the FDA and World Health Organization reason to more actively intervene to regulate the tobacco industry. This has been a slow

In October 1995, someone calling himself "a concerned citizen" who "cannot sign my name because it would place my family at risk" mailed an internal tobacco industry memo to the FDA. The memo was written in 1972 by Claude Teague, RJ Reynolds's assistant research director, and said that smokers chose a cigarette brand mainly because of "individual nicotine dosage requirements and [only] secondarily by a variety of other considerations, including flavor." He continued, "A tobacco product is, in essence, a vehicle for delivering nicotine. Happily for the tobacco industry, nicotine is both habituating [habit-forming] and unique in its variety of physiological actions."

process because of the power of the tobacco industry but in 2005, a global treaty was put into force to begin the process of regulating tobacco trade and manufacture as never before.

This process was jumpstarted in the United States when the National Institute on Drug Abuse (NIDA) tested nicotine to see if it truly met the standards for an addictive drug. By the early 1980s, the answer was a definitive "yes." In fact, the studies showed that milligram for milligram, nicotine was 5 to 10 times more potent than cocaine. By 1988, the US Surgeon General reported that nicotine was an addictive drug, as powerful, in many ways as cocaine and heroin, and causing much more death and disease. As evidence of nicotine's addictive power accumulated in the 1980s and 1990s, tobacco companies grew increasingly defensive. They claimed that nicotine was a "flavor molecule," and asked how smoking could be addictive if so many smokers had successfully quit. Tobacco companies also called into question the definition of "addictive," criticizing the U.S. Food and Drug Administration (FDA) for comparing nicotine "addiction" to cocaine "addiction," and claimed the two are significantly different.

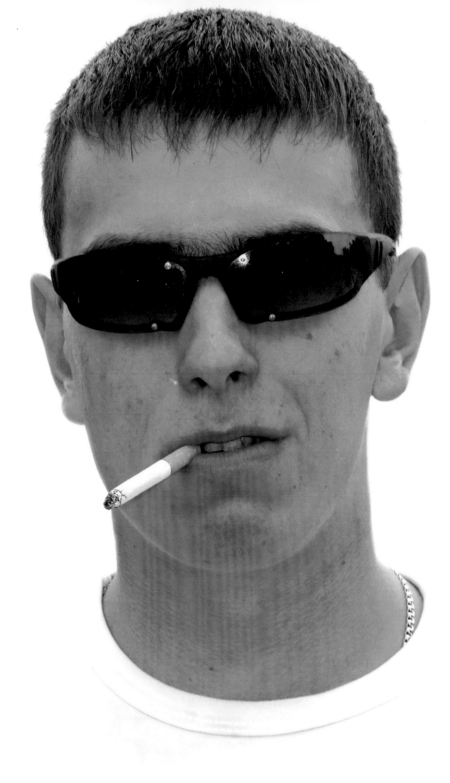

Smoking may make young adults feel "cool," but nicotine is particularly dangerous for young adults.

Tobacco and Your Body

It's hard for many young people to imagine themselves forty years from now. In fact, many young people believe cigarettes are only harmful to the middle-aged and elderly. While it is true that cigarettes often take the lives of older rather than younger people, tobacco begins doing damage much earlier—from the very first drag on a cigarette.

What Smoking Does While You're Still Young

Your heart rate rises 30 percent during the first ten minutes of smoking, and it continues to increase with each subsequent cigarette, increasing your blood pressure as well. Cigarettes also narrow blood vessels, inhibiting the body's blood supply.

This causes many problems for a young smoker. Because oxygen supply is reduced, a young athlete's performance and endurance suffer significantly. Decreased blood flow also results in "smoker's face"—a pale, gray pallor; one cigarette can reduce the blood supply to the skin for more than an hour. Smokers experience shortness of breath almost three times more often than nonsmokers.

Smoking also makes teens and preteens more susceptible to colds and asthma attacks; one in three people treated for asthma attacks in emergency rooms are smokers. Sports, singing, and dancing are often out of the picture for young people who choose to smoke. Athletes and dancers who smoke will have to work twice as hard to offset their diminished oxygen supply, and singers will suffer dry, scorched vocal chords.

For some young people, the cosmetic effects of smoking are the worst effects of smoking: yellow teeth, smelly

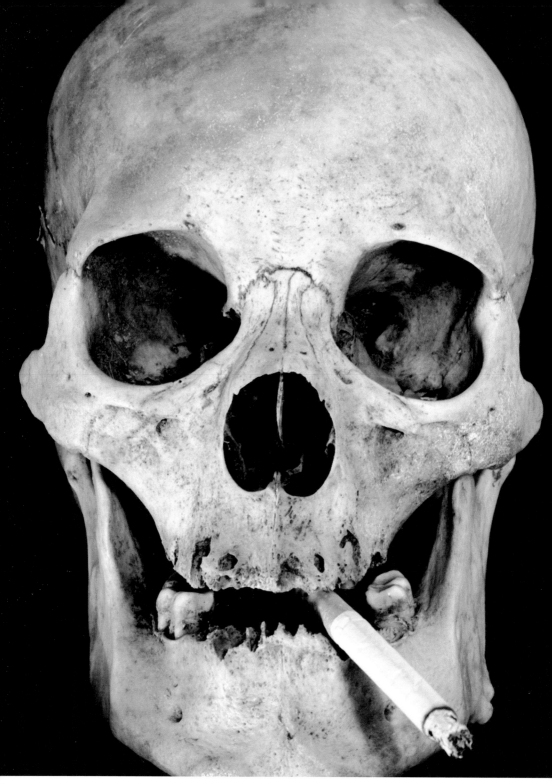

Nicotine is a hazardous chemical that can cause death in variety of ways.

clothes and hair, and bad breath are all part of a smoker's new image.

Smoking and Your Brain

Once you inhale the smoke from a cigarette or cigar, the nicotine reaches your brain in only a few seconds—and once in the brain, nicotine affects communication between the brain's cells, the neurons. Neurons are responsible for receiving and transmitting messages from other neurons, but they can't do the job alone. They use chemical messengers known as neurotransmitters to carry these messages from neuron to neuron within the brain. Nicotine acts on a specific type of neurotransmitter called acetylcholine, which delivers signals from your brain to your muscles, controls your energy level, controls how fast your heart beats and how often you take a breath, oversees the flow of information throughout your brain (how fast and how slow messages are transmitted between neurons), and enables you to learn and remember things.

Nicotine increases the amount of acetylcholine in the brain, which increases the amount of messages transmitted between brain cells. This causes an almost immediate feeling of alertness in the smoker, a rise in energy level, and what seems like an increased ability to pay attention or focus.

Nicotine also increases how much of a second neurotransmitter, called dopamine, is released in the brain. Dopamine works in the part of your brain responsible for survival instincts (eating and reproduction, for example), happy feelings, and pleasurable sensations. It is sometimes called "the pleasure molecule." It is the same neurotransmitter affected by highly addictive drugs like heroin and cocaine. An increase in dopamine is what many smokers experience as peaceful, pleasurable, calm feelings.

Dopamine levels are also considered the root of most chemical addictions.

In addition to neurotransmitters, nicotine can cause your brain to increase production of endorphins, your body's painkilling proteins. These natural analgesics (painkillers) can cause feelings of *euphoria*—like a runner's high—and reduce awareness of pain. More pleasure; less pain—no wonder people enjoy smoking!

The downside of nicotine is that its effect on the brain doesn't last. The brain cries out for more nicotine as soon as thirty minutes after finishing a cigarette. That's why many teen smokers admit to feeling nicotine cravings even after trying only one or two cigarettes. The good feelings nicotine supplies are short-lived, requiring the tobacco user to use tobacco products more and more to get the same "high."

Another downside of nicotine is that some of the neurotransmitters responsible for nicotine's energetic feelings or short-term highs are the same neurotransmitters involved in anxiety disorders and depression. A recent study published in the *Journal of the American Medical Association* found that teen smokers became more prone to generalized **anxiety disorders**, panic attacks, and agoraphobia (fear of public places) than their nonsmoking peers. In another article the American Psychological Association, quoting a study published in Pediatrics magazine, reported that smoking was the single strongest predictor of a teen's developing depressive symptoms. Among nondepressed teens, those who smoked were four times more likely to develop depression than those who did not.

Tobacco and the Rest of Your Body

Inhaled nicotine, the addictive chemical in tobacco, doesn't only impact the brain; it works on other areas of

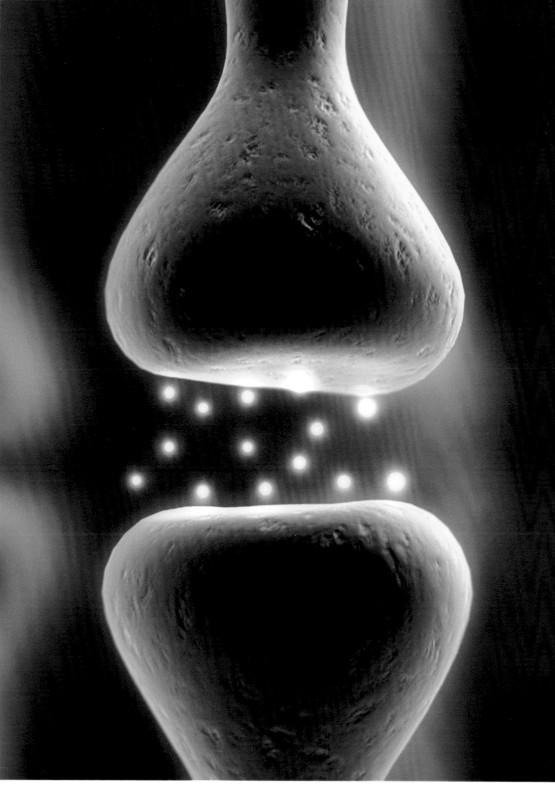

Nicotine interferes with the neurotransmitters that carry messages between nerve cells within the brain.

the body. At first, nicotine causes your body to release a hormone called adrenaline—the same hormone that is triggered by fear. Most of us have experienced an "adrenaline rush" when riding a particularly frightening roller coaster, when terrified by a scary movie, or when nearly being involved in a traffic accident. Adrenaline causes your heart to beat faster, your breathing rate to increase, and your blood pressure to rise. Nicotine has the same effect.

While it's causing a release of adrenaline, inhaled nicotine simultaneously blocks the release of another hormone called insulin. Too little insulin results in higher levels of sugar in your blood—a condition called hyperglycemia—so that your body cuts back on its demand for food. This causes the reduced appetite many smokers experience.

What Smoking Does Over the Long Run

Both in the United States and Canada, smoking is the number-one cause of preventable illness. Death caused by smoking is most often the result of a lifetime of addiction to tobacco.

Tobacco-related cancers can occur nearly anywhere in the body's major systems, but they tend to occur more frequently in those areas that have direct contact with tobacco's chemicals. The most common tobacco-related cancers occur in the mouth, throat, and lungs.

Cancers of the Mouth

Cancers of the mouth, also known as oral cancers, are particularly brutal. According to the Oral Cancer Foundation (www.oralcancerfoundation.org), close to 40,000 Americans are diagnosed with oral or pharyngeal (can-

HOW SMOKING HARMS YOUR BODY

Brain and Mental Effects
- strokes (cerebrovascular accidents)
- addiction / withdrawal
- altered brain chemistry
- increased anxiety

Nose
- damaged sense of smell

Teeth
- discoloration and stains
- plaque
- loose teeth
- gum disease (gingivitis)

Mouth and Throat
- cancers of lips, mouth, throat, and larynx
- chronic sore throat
- reduced sense of taste
- bad breath

Respiration and Lungs
- lung cancer
- cough and sputum, shortness of breath
- colds and flu, pneumonia, asthma
- chronic obstructive pulmonary disease and emphysema
- complicates tuberculosis

Liver
- cancer

Kidneys and Bladder
- cancer

Male Reproduction
- sperm: deformity, loss of motility, reduced number
- infertility
- impotence

Legs and Feet
- increased leg pain and gangrene
- peripheral vascular disease
- Buerger's disease

Hair
- bad odor and staining

Eyes
- eyes sting, water, and blink more frequently
- blindness (macular degeneration)
- cataracts

Skin
- wrinkling
- premature aging

Chest
- cancer of esophagus

Heart
- harms, blocks, and weakens arteries of the heart
- heart attacks

Abdomen
- stomach and duodenal ulcers
- cancers of the stomach, pancreas, colon
- aortic aneurysm

Hands
- poor circulation (cold/sore fingers)
- peripheral vascular disease
- tar-stained fingers

Female Reproduction
- menstrual pains
- earlier menopause
- cancer of cervix
- infertility and delay of conception
- low birth weight
- increased chance of spontaneous abortion

Bones
- osteoporosis
- spine and hip fractures

Wounds and Surgery
- wounds take longer to heal
- surgical recovery time longer

Diabetes
- noninsulin dependent diabetes mellitus (Type 2, adult onset)

Immune System
- severely weakened

Blood
- leukemia

(Source: Smoking 101)

The Big Risk: Cancer

According to the American Cancer Society:

Cancer develops when cells in a part of the body begin to grow out of control. Although there are many kinds of cancer, they all start because of out-of-control growth of abnormal cells.... Because cancer cells continue to grow and divide, they are different from normal cells. Instead of dying, they outlive normal cells and continue to form new abnormal cells.

Cancer cells develop because of damage to DNA.... People can inherit damaged DNA, which accounts for inherited cancers. Many times though, a person's DNA becomes damaged by exposure to something in the environment, like smoking.

cers of the pharynx, which is located between the mouth and the esophagus) cancers each year. Less than half of these will still be alive five years after their diagnoses. Oral cancer kills one person every hour, twenty-four hours a day, every year. Seventy-five percent of these, or three out of four, are tobacco users.

In its earliest stages, oral cancer can look like less serious conditions. It can show up as a white or red spot on your tongue, under your tongue, or the inside of your cheek. It might look like an acid pimple, a common canker sore, or a cold sore on your lips. Sometimes it will appear as a solid lump that you can feel inside your mouth, tongue, or neck. It can also seem like a bad case of laryngitis, a hoarseness that just won't quit. Other times, the first symptoms may be pain, numbness, or difficulty when you swallow, talk, or eat. In later stages, it can look like a bumpy wart at the very back of your mouth, either on your tongue or near your tonsils.

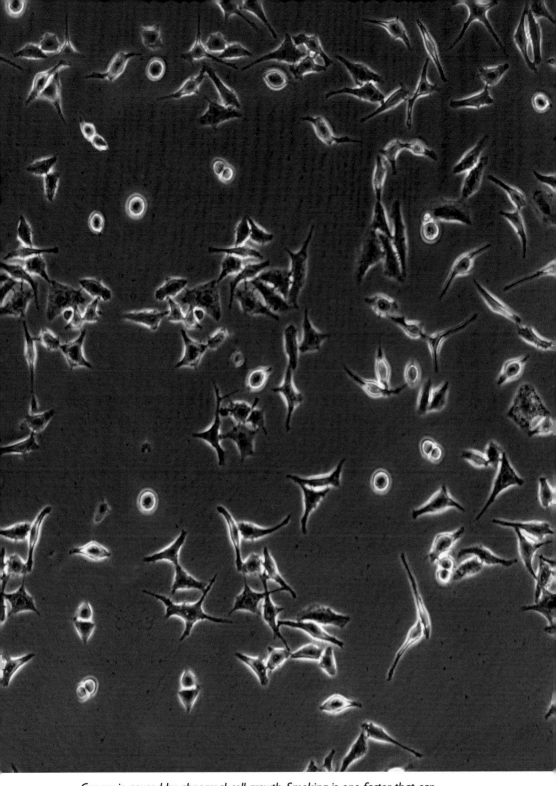

Cancer is caused by abnormal cell growth. Smoking is one factor that can stimulate this often-fatal condition.

FAST FACT

Cigarette smoking causes at least 30 percent of all cancer deaths. It causes 87 percent of lung cancer deaths, and over 90 percent of oral (mouth) and laryngeal (voice box) cancers.

The treatment of oral cancer usually involves some combination of surgery, radiation therapy (where cancer cells are bombarded with high doses of radiation in an effort to kill them), and chemotherapy (where cancer cells are "poisoned" with certain chemicals in an attempt to kill them). Surgical treatment for oral cancer is almost always necessary and is often disfiguring. Imagine what you would look like without your jawbone or neck muscles. Imagine how difficult it would be to eat if you only had half of your tongue.

Cancers of the Throat

Tobacco smokers, sniffers, and chewers all put their throats in direct contact with the tobacco products they use. The two parts of the throat most commonly affected by the chemicals in tobacco are the esophagus (the tube that runs from the back of the mouth to the stomach) and the larynx (the voice box). Cancer can develop in both: esophageal cancer is cancer of the esophagus, and laryngeal cancer is cancer of the larynx.

The National Cancer Institute estimates that over 12,000 people are diagnosed with laryngeal cancer per year, or about thirty people per day. The American Cancer Society estimates that in the same time period, over 17,000 new cases of esophageal cancers will be diagnosed, or 46 people per day. And that's just in the United States. Other countries, like China, Iran, India, and southern parts of Africa where smoking is far more prevalent and acceptable, have ten to one hundred times more esophageal cancer cases per year than the United States.

FAST FACT

Each year cancer kills more young people under twenty years of age than asthma, diabetes, AIDS, and cystic fibrosis combined!

Smoking is as deadly as any plague.

Real People with Cancer

Read these online stories of people who faced tobacco-related cancers:

- former pro baseball player Rick Bender, now known as "the Man Without a Face"
  www.nosnuff.com/bio.html

- nineteen-year-old former track star Sean Marsee (now deceased)
  whyquit.com/whyquit/SeanMarsee.html

- twenty-five-year-old oral cancer survivor Gruen Von Behrens
  whyquit.com/whyquit\A_Gruen.html

One of the most difficult aspects of laryngeal cancer for patients to handle (apart from the threat of death) is having their larynx removed as part of their treatment. The larynx contains the vocal cords, which give sound to your voice. Without vocal cords, you lose your ability to talk as you once did. Patients who have their voice boxes removed have to learn to talk in a different way. They never sound the same again. These patients also lose much of their sense of taste and smell.

Over 90 percent of laryngeal cancers are caused by smoking tobacco products.

FAST FACT

Smoking a pack and a half of cigarettes per day for a year exposes the lining of the lungs to same amount of radiation (from the lead in tobacco leaves) as would be found in having 1,600 chest X-rays.

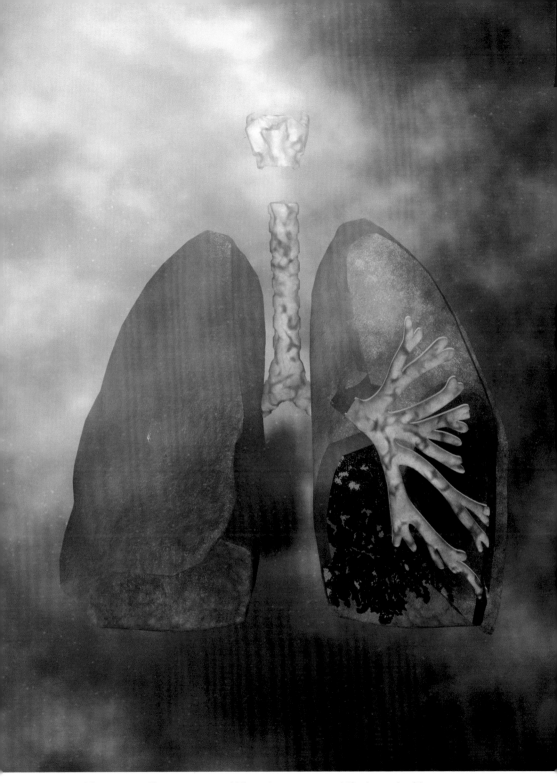

Most cases of lung cancer could have been prevented if tobacco had been avoided.

Limiting contact with tobacco products greatly reduces your risk of developing either of these deadly diseases.

Lung Cancer

Though using tobacco products can cause many types of cancer, including mouth and throat cancers, lung cancer is the cancer most commonly associated with smoking.

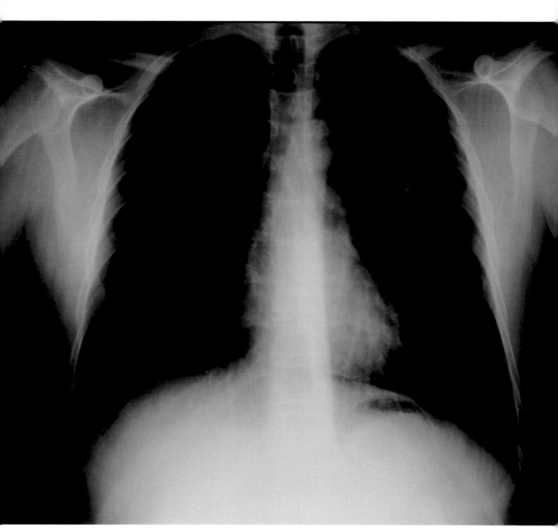

Lung cancer invades the lungs, leaving fewer healthy cells to take in oxygen.

Cigarette Smoking-Related Mortality

1. Between 1960 and 1990, deaths from lung cancer among women have increased by more than 400 percent, exceeding breast cancer deaths by the mid-1980s. The American Cancer Society estimated that in 2010, 71,080 women died from lung cancer and 39,840 died from breast cancer.

2. Men who smoke increase their risk of death from lung cancer by more than twenty-two times and from bronchitis and emphysema by nearly ten times. Women who smoke increase their risk of dying from lung cancer by nearly twelve times and the risk of dying from bronchitis and emphysema by more than ten times. Smoking triples the risk of dying from heart disease among middle-aged men and women.

3. Every year in the United States, premature deaths from smoking rob more than five million years from the potential lifespan of those who have died.

4. Annually, exposure to secondhand smoke (or environmental tobacco smoke) causes an estimated three thousand deaths from lung cancer among American adults. Scientific studies also link secondhand smoke with heart disease.

[Source: Centers for Disease Control and Prevention (CDC)]

It makes up almost one-fourth of all cancer deaths. That means that one out of every four people who die from any form of cancer dies from lung cancer. Nearly 90 percent of all lung cancers are caused by smoking.

Think of it this way: if you knew that in forty years an awful plague was going to come and wipe out over 160,000 people your age, and you had a secret formula that would keep nearly 140,000 of them alive, wouldn't you do something to save them? Wouldn't you give the formula to as many people as you could? Wouldn't you take the formula yourself to keep from dying?

Lung cancer is most often diagnosed in people between the ages of fifty-five and seventy—today's teenagers in roughly forty years. The American Cancer Society estimates that lung cancer will kill over 160,000 adults each year. Seven out of eight of these deaths are entirely preventable. Nearly 140,000 of these adults can be saved. The solution is simple: don't use tobacco products. If all the people predicted to die from future lung cancer deaths caused by smoking chose not to smoke, over 140,000 lives could be saved per year.

This kind of cancer begins in the lungs. The right lung has three sections, called lobes. The left lung, which allows room for the heart, only has two. The lungs are what enable us to inhale and exhale and move air in and

More Deadly Statistics

- Eighty to 90 percent of people with chronic obstructive pulmonary disease (COPD)—a group of lung diseases—have a history of significant tobacco use.
- The CDC estimates that men and women who smoke are ten times more likely to die of bronchitis and emphysema than those who stay smoke-free.
- The U.S. Department of Health and Human Services affirms that the risk of stroke in people who smoke is 50 percent higher than those who do not.
- The CDC also estimates that tobacco use triples your risk of dying from heart disease and doubles your risk of sudden cardiac death (heart attack).
- The U.S. Surgeon General views cigarette smoking as so dangerous to heart health, in fact, that he calls it "the most important of the modifiable risk factors for coronary heart disease in the United States."

Almost half a million people die from cigarette smoking each year in the United States.

out of our bodies. When we inhale, we take in good air, which contains needed oxygen, and when we exhale, we get rid of bad air, a waste product called carbon dioxide.

For air to get into our bodies, it must travel down the windpipe into the lungs. The single windpipe divides into two tubes called bronchi (forming a kind of upside-down "Y"), each of which leads to a lung. Once in the lung, the bronchi divide into smaller branches called bronchioles, in the same way that tree branches divide and get smaller as you go further out the limbs. At the end of these small branches are tiny air sacs called alveoli. It's in these air sacs, kind of like leaves on a tree, where our bodies exchange carbon dioxide (the bad air we exhale) for oxygen (that we inhale).

Most lung cancers affect the bronchi first, but they can also start in other places such as the trachea, bronchioles, or alveoli. Wherever it starts invading healthy respiratory tissue cells with the uncontrolled growth of cancer's abnormal cells, lung cancer makes it progressively harder to breathe and get the oxygen the body needs. Death from lung cancer is often like long, slow suffocation that can take months or even years.

Treatments for lung cancer vary depending on type of lung cancer, its severity, and when it is diagnosed. Like other cancers, most lung cancers are treated with a com-

Although smoking is often portrayed as glamorous and sexy, its reality is anything but.

Celebrities Who Died From Tobacco-Related Cancers

Babe Ruth (baseball player), of throat cancer at age 53
Carl Wilson (of the Beach Boys), of lung cancer at age 51
Michael Landon (actor), of pancreatic cancer at age 54
Walt Disney, of lung cancer at age 65
Carrie Hamilton (actress Carol Burnett's daughter),
　　of lung cancer at age 38
Sammy Davis Jr. (singer/entertainer), of throat cancer at age 64
Nat "King" Cole (musician), of lung cancer at age 45
Luiz Jose Costa (Brazilian music star), of lung cancer at age 36
Eric Carr (drummer for KISS), of lung cancer at age 41
Graham Chapman (of Monty Python), of throat cancer at age 48
Humphrey Bogart (actor), of esophageal cancer at age 57
Sigmund Freud (psychoanalyst), of oral cancer at age 83

bination of surgery (to remove the cancerous part of the lungs), radiation therapy, and chemotherapy. Despite these efforts, most people do not survive lung cancer. Of those who are diagnosed with lung cancer, only 40 percent (only two out of five) will still be alive a year later. And only one out of ten (roughly 13 percent) will be alive five years after they are diagnosed.

Overwhelming Evidence

Cancer also causes other diseases besides cancer, including heart disease and high blood pressure. In recent years, the CDC in the United States and the Public Health Agency of Canada have compiled vast amounts of information on mortality and disease related to smoking.

In Canada, for example, smoking is the cause of one-fifth of all deaths from cancer. Over 47,000 Canadians die each year from smoking. In 1996, cigarette smoking was

Smoking need not be a death sentence. The sooner you quit, the better!

responsible for 26 percent of male deaths and 16 percent of female deaths. There is increasing concern in Canada for teenage smokers; government programs in the past decade have done much to combat the prevalence of smoking among Canadian youth. These efforts seem to have been successful, as smoking among youth and adults has steadily decreased in the past five years. Even so, there is much to be done in Canada to reduce smoking-related deaths.

In the United States, cigarette smoking is the single most preventable cause of premature death. Each year, more than 440,000 Americans die from cigarette smoking. In fact, one in every five deaths in the United States is smoking related. Every year, smoking kills more than 270,000 men and over 170,000 women.

As you read these facts and figures, it may be hard to remember that these numbers represent real people, with real friends, families, and lives. Books like this—packed full of information and harsh warnings against cigarettes—can seem overwhelming. Sometimes, you may feel as though you've heard it all so often, that you no longer want to pay attention. But this message is true: smoking can kill you.

One Woman's Story

On the website quitsmoking.about.com, one woman shares her story:

Hi Everyone,

My name is Cheryl, and I have been here before in one of my many attempts to stop smoking. I believe I lasted 3 months last time.

I caught pneumonia in October 2003. When I saw my X-rays, I knew. The doctors still wanted more tests and **biopsies**, but the fact was plain as day when I saw the X-rays. I believe I knew months before that I had cancer, but I would not let myself think about it.

I was diagnosed with limited **small-cell** lung cancer and **squamous third-stage B** on November 19, 2003. It's **inoperable** and incurable. I had finally pushed my luck as far as my body could handle.

Now my life and my family's lives are very stressful, painful, expensive and inconvenient for everyone. I have to drive over 100 miles a day to go to radiation treatments 5 days a week, with weekends and holidays off. . . . I do this for 5 weeks with 2 weeks off, and then 2 more weeks of radiation. It hurts and burns. It gives me spasms that are as painful as heart attacks. I got **thrush** from the chemotherapy, and at times I can't even swallow water. I have to be driven by someone who loses that many hours a day of their life/work time because I am too ill and tired to drive myself.

I will do 4 rounds of chemotherapy during the radiation process—chemo 3 days, every 3 weeks. It's pure poison, and it makes me so ill I can't breathe, eat, or drink sometimes. When all of these treatments are completed, and if I live through it, they will test me to see what the cancers have done. They will have either grown more and gone to my brain, liver, or bones, or—if I am fortunate enough to be blessed—they will be gone.

Sadly, Cheryl did not win her battle with cancer. She died on June 30, 2005. Like so many smokers, Cheryl was fatally wounded by cigarettes. She was a courageous and loving person, but tobacco is an impersonal opponent, indifferent to personality or charisma.

But if you smoke, you don't have to die. There are other options.

5 Kicking the Habit

Perhaps you've already started smoking, and you need help quitting. If so, you're not alone. Each year, 17 million smokers in the United States attempt to quit smoking. Unfortunately, only about 8 percent of those who try to quit will succeed.

Are You Serious About Quitting?

The first step is to make a decision to quit. Smokers everywhere will often joke, "Yeah, I quit last month" as they drag on a fresh cigarette. For many people addicted to cigarettes, making the decision to quit is sometimes a longer process than quitting itself. The amount of information available to smokers today is reason enough to quit, however. Increasing government regulation of tobacco is another helpful asset in the fight against tobacco. But addiction remains—even with more smokers than ever before ready to quit.

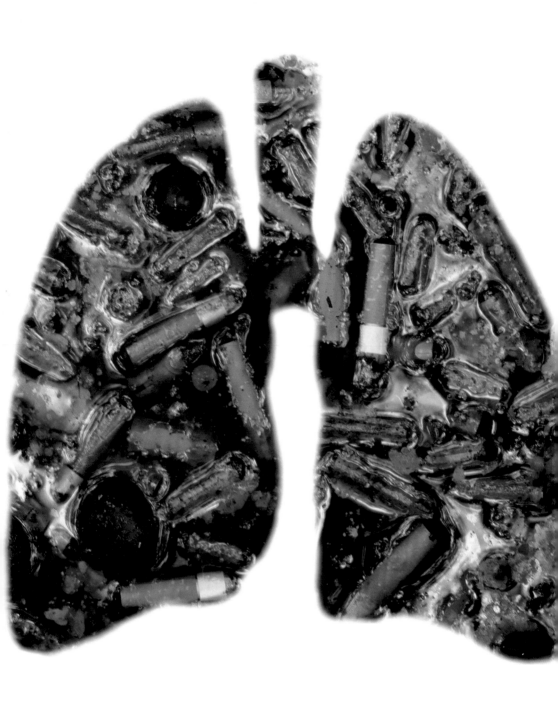

Your lungs will thank you if you quit smoking.

Quitting is well worth the effort. Within twenty minutes after you smoke that last cigarette, your body begins a series of changes that continue for years.

- Twenty minutes after your last cigarette, your heart rate drops.
- Twelve hours after quitting, the carbon monoxide level in your blood drops to normal.
- Two weeks to three months after quitting, your heart attack risk begins to drop, and your lung function begins to improve.
- One to nine months after quitting, your coughing and shortness of breath decrease.
- One year after quitting, your added risk of coronary heart disease is half that of a smoker's.
- Five years after quitting, your stroke risk is reduced to that of a nonsmoker's.
- Ten years after quitting, your lung cancer death rate is about half that of a smoker's; your risk of cancers of the mouth, throat, esophagus, bladder, kidney, and pancreas also decreases.
- Fifteen years after quitting, your risk of coronary heart disease is back to that of a nonsmoker's.

Helping Youth Quit

One of the first steps to quitting is taking your addiction seriously. Many cigarette smokers have admitted to embarrassment over quitting; it can be an extremely difficult time, as both physiological and emotional changes occur. Nicotine addiction is as serious as any other addiction; it's important to remind yourself of that.

If you want to quit smoking, get the support and information you'll need to help you.

Quitting can be an even more daunting for a young person than for an older person. The world of help for young smokers is more vague. The young smoker must remember, first of all, that quitting smoking requires a system of help, not one solution. Research has shown poor results for smoking intervention programs that focus on one method only.

Consider this framework of steps when quitting:

1. Establish self-awareness of tobacco use
2. Establish motivation to quit
3. Prepare for quitting
4. Establish strategies to maintain abstinence

Establish Self-Awareness

Quitting cigarettes is so difficult largely because of the drug nicotine. Quitting will become even more difficult, however, if nicotine isn't taken seriously. Many Canadian cigarette packages warn: "Cigarettes are highly addictive. Studies have shown that tobacco can be harder to quit than heroin or cocaine."

If you are a young smoker, consider this checklist from Margaret Hyde's book, *Smoking 101*:

1. Have you ever tried to quit but couldn't?
2. Do you smoke now because it is really hard to quit?
3. Have you ever felt you were addicted to tobacco?
4. Do you ever have strong cravings to smoke?
5. Have you ever felt as if you really *needed* a cigarette?
6. Is it hard not smoking in places that prohibit smoking?

7. When you tried to stop smoking (or when you haven't used tobacco for a while), did you find it hard to concentrate?

If you're answering yes to most of these questions, than you need to be aware: you are addicted to tobacco. Facing that realization is a vital first step toward self-awareness.

"No Light Smoking"

Many people consider themselves safe from harm because they are social or casual smokers. They smoke only with friends at a party or have a few cigarettes after dinner. This sense of safety is an illusion. New studies have shown that just one or two cigarettes a day can limit the ability of blood vessels to dilate, causing dangerous plaque buildup. In 2002, Susan Brink investigated this matter in her article "No Light Smoking." In the article, John Ambrose, medical director of St. Vincent's Medical Center in New York City, reports that light smokers show the same damage as heavy smokers.

Motivation to Quit

The next step is preparing motivation. Most young people have a variety of reasons they would like to quit. Here are just a few that real teens offered:

- I'm tired of trying to hide my smoking from a parent, friend, or girlfriend/boyfriend. I'm tired of using mints, perfume, and body lotion to cover up cigarette stink.
- I don't want to smell like an ashtray.
- If I want to date him/her, I need to stop smoking.

- Money, money, money! (Money is one of the most common reasons for quitting. Higher taxes on cigarettes are highly effective in reducing the demand for cigarettes.)
- My life is scheduled around cigarettes: when I don't have one, it's almost unbearable.
- I want deep, full breaths of air again. I want to be able to run hard and fast.
- I want to smell things again.
- Smoking is dangerous. My grandmother has cancer from smoking.
- I want white teeth.

Every time you feel like picking up a cigarette, pick up this list instead. Keep it with you. You'll need constant reminders during this process. Remember, though: you're not alone.

Prepare to Quit

Set the Date

Choose a quit day. Planning ahead for quitting will be extremely helpful later, when cravings begin. Millions of people choose to quit for a day or longer on the third Thursday of November. This is a day celebrated annually as The Great American Smokeout, sponsored by the American Cancer Society originally in 1976 in California, and now nationally endorsed.

Another quit day is sponsored by the World Health Organization (WHO) to call attention to cigarettes' global impact on health. It is called the World No Tobacco Day, celebrated each year on May 31, and can differ from country to country, but the goal is always the same: quitting smoking.

But you don't have to wait for one of these holidays to quit. Don't let yourself off the hook if these dates are more than a week or two away. You need to begin before you lose motivation. Choose a day within the next week, and celebrate that day as a personal holiday each year.

Prep Work

Stop buying cigarettes. Tell your family about your decision, and inform them of the upcoming changes in your life. Your friends and family should know about your decision, and you should consider asking for their support. Remind them that you may experience changes in mood, but that it won't last long. The worst will be over soon.

Keep a journal. Make a list of "triggers" that urge you to smoke. Also note things that seem to complement a cigarette—coffee, soda, talking on the phone, hanging out with certain friends—and try to avoid those later.

Find cigarette replacements: toothpicks, chewing gum, anything that might serve as a physical replacement for a cigarette.

Make plans for money you will save by not smoking; make a list of phone numbers you'll call if you need support or reminders.

Throw out all cigarettes. Throw out cigarettes stashed in drawers, cabinets, and tins; you'll need to get rid of any temptations. Plan on leaving the room

FAST FACT

50 percent of teenage smokers in United States reported trying to quit in 2007. More Female students (55 percent) reported trying to quit than male students (45 percent).

Peer pressure often plays a role in how hard or easy a person finds kicking the habit.

when others smoke. Ask friends and family not to smoke around you.

Nicotine-Replacement Treatments

Research has shown that drug treatments for nicotine do work. Over-the-counter availability of these medications—along with media messages to quit smoking—have increased the rate of successful quitting each year by 20 percent. They roughly double the odds that a person will be able to achieve lasting abstinence from cigarettes. However, they have not been studied much in young people, and therefore, the FDA advises that a doctor be involved in their use with persons under eighteen, including when considering using over-the-counter medicines such as nicotine gum, lozenges, and patches.

Nicotine gum was the first drug approved by the FDA for use in smoking cessation therapy. Nicotine replacement therapies include: nicotine gum, lozenge, the **transdermal** patch (commonly called "the patch"), nicotine nasal spray, and nicotine inhaler. These are just the therapies approved in the United States and Canada; there are countless other varieties being developed and sold in other parts of the world. These nicotine-replacement products are designed to ease withdrawal symptoms. They are safe alternatives to tobacco and provide lower overall nicotine levels. These forms of treatment have little potential for abuse, because they provide none of the other pleasures of cigarettes. According to U.S. government research, all the nicotine-replacement products—gum, patch, spray, and inhaler—appear to be equally effective.

Non-Nicotine Therapy

In the past decade, researchers and physicians have concentrated on behavioral therapies to combat addiction.

The U.S. government report at www.drugabuse.gov says these behavioral methods are used to:

a. define high-risk relapse situations,
b. create an aversion to smoking,
c. develop self-monitoring of smoking behavior, and
d. establish competing coping responses.

The report also states:

> Other key factors in successful treatment include avoiding smokers and smoking environments and receiving support from family and friends. The single most important factor, however, may be the learning and use of coping skills for both short- and long-term prevention of relapse. Smokers must not only learn behavioral and cognitive tools for relapse prevention but must also be ready to apply those skills in a crisis.

These methods are powerful when used alone, but prove to be much more effective when combined with nicotine-replacement therapies like the patch or gum. A young man who uses the patch and attends a support group, for instance, has a much better chance of successfully quitting. Nonetheless, anyone who quits smoking can plan on facing several hurdles.

There is also an antidepressant (buproprion or Zyban®) and nicotine-like drug varenicline (Chantix®) that are being used to treat nicotine addiction. Other medicines, including vaccines, are under development. The nicotine-replacement products are designed to aid quitting and reduce withdrawal symptoms by providing nicotine in a form that is safe when used as directed. According

A variety of techniques are available to help you quit smoking, including nicotine-replacement therapies, behavioral methods, and abstinence strategies.

to U.S. government research, all of the FDA approved medicines are about equally effective, roughly doubling the odds of success. But, as is the case with other kinds of medicines, individuals have different preferences and responses to different medicines. Sometimes people need to try more than one to find the one that is right for them.

Abstinence Strategies

Hurdle #1: Nicotine Withdrawal

We saw in earlier chapters that nicotine is a highly addictive chemical found in tobacco, and that when smoke is inhaled, nicotine is carried to the lungs, then into the bloodstream, and to the brain where it affects chemical neurotransmitters. Nicotine actually changes your brain's chemical makeup. As you get used to having nicotine in your body, you tend to need more of the drug to satisfy your cravings for it, until your body adapts to a higher level of nicotine in your blood and brain. In other words, your body gets used to having nicotine in its system and adapts. Then it wants more.

When you suddenly take nicotine away, your body craves it, making you feel like you need to have more nicotine or you'll die or get sick or something drastic will happen. When that craving is frustrated, your body rebels with all kinds of symptoms: headaches, fatigue, trouble sleeping, trouble paying attention, irritability, feelings of anger and frustration, anxiety, depression, hunger, thirst, agitation, and the jitters. These symptoms can be quite severe, and can appear in just a few short hours after your last cigarette. They will be at their worst two to three days later if you don't smoke at all during that time, and can last for weeks. Sometimes withdrawal symptoms are so bad people feel like they have no choice but to smoke to ease their discomfort. This is why so many people try to quit and fail.

This immediate and complete removal of nicotine from smokers is called quitting "cold turkey." It means choosing to stop and never smoking again without any help or intervention. While admirable, this approach will work for only some people. Because nicotine is such a powerful substance, others might need to be tapered off it slowly.

Slowly reducing the number of cigarettes you smoke in a day can be a means of tapering off, but the many nicotine-replacement products available on the market today make that unnecessary.

Trying to gradually decrease the number of cigarettes you smoke each day can be a surprisingly hard option. Nicotine-replacement products offer greater chances of success.

Hurdle #2: Psychological Dependence

Smokers don't just depend on nicotine physically. They depend on it behaviorally and psychologically. Smoking can be the thing you do when you get together with friends. It may be your means to blow off steam when you feel tense. Lighting up may be part of your family culture. Quitting means that all those things will have to change in some way, at least for you. It's not easy.

One way to make the transition easier is to be prepared. How will you handle your urges to put something in your mouth, for example? Try gum, hard candy, lollipops, crunchy raw vegetables, nuts, or flavored toothpicks. What about when you're angry? Maybe rather than lighting up, you can go for a run instead. The idea is to replace the former behavior with a new, different, healthier-for-you behavior.

Here's another example. If you know that you're tempted to smoke when you're bored, plan to be extremely busy for the first few days after you quit: get together with nonsmoking friends, go shopping, work extra hours, do hand crafts, play a musical instrument, have a video-game marathon, take in a double feature at the movie theater, go to the local gym, add an extra workout, go out of town, take a camping trip. Again, replace the smoking behavior with something new and pleasurable.

Try changing your routine or doing something you haven't done before. Take a class at the public library or local YMCA. Join a fitness club. Investigate a new committee or team at school. Volunteer at your local hospital, library, or other place where smoking is not allowed. Get a different part-time job. The excitement and newness of the change will keep you from becoming bored and restless.

If you know that a certain circle of friends pressures you to smoke, make arrangements to hang out with different, nonsmoking friends for the first two weeks after you quit. Then practice how you'll handle your smoking friends before you put yourself in that situation.

You should also understand what are called the "recovery symptoms" of smoking withdrawal. Familiarize yourself with the effects of withdrawal.

Hurdle #3: Maintaining Your Change

Many former smokers are able to quit for one day or one week or even one month. But becoming permanently nicotine-free requires work and diligence. Here are a few strategies that might help for the long haul (adapted from the American Cancer Society's Guide for Quitting Smoking):

1. Try positive self-talk. Tell yourself the truth. When the cravings are at their worst, remind yourself that even though they feel overwhelming right now, they won't last forever. The craving will pass. That's true.
2. Recognize false self-talk, also called "rationalization." Thoughts like *If I don't smoke I can't have fun* or *One little cigarette won't hurt, will it?* are simply not true. Recognize them for the lies or false beliefs they are, and then abandon them.
3. Avoid situations where you are most tempted to smoke. You know best what these may be. Maybe it's a certain group of friends or school activity or hang out. Stay away from these until you're sure you can handle them without smoking.

RECOVERY SYMPTOMS

Many people say they feel different both physically and mentally once they quit smoking. All these symptoms decrease sharply during the first few days of quitting smoking. Afterwards, these symptoms will continue to decline more slowly through the next two to four weeks. So as you stay off cigarettes, you will feel better and better.

Craving

The physical addiction to nicotine diminishes after a week to ten days, but it is a highly variable craving that can also resurge even after years.

Sleepiness/Irritability

Nicotine is a stimulant that peps you up and speeds up your circulation. Your body is adjusting to the loss of nicotine in the body. It is healing itself. You may notice that you feel tired more in mid-afternoon.

Headaches

You're not getting as much blood and oxygen to the brain when the circulation goes down. It may take several weeks before you feel normal. See your health care provider about how to manage these headaches.

Depressed

It's common to feel depressed after quitting. Some people feel like they've lost a close friend. Bouts of crying may occur. These feelings will pass. Starting to smoke again is NOT the answer. In fact, smoking may trigger feelings of failure and guilt that make you feel even worse.

Stomach Problems

Intestinal movement may slow down for a brief time (usually one to two weeks). This may cause constipation and gas pains.

Coughing

This may not be related to nicotine withdrawal. This is the body's way of getting rid of mucous and tar that blocked airways and reduced breathing. This will last only a few days after quitting.

Dizziness

This is also not related to nicotine withdrawal. Occasional dizziness is caused by extra oxygen your body is getting. This will subside in one to two days after quitting.

Lack of Concentration

The ex-smoker needs time to adjust to a routine of not having the stimulation of nicotine. Most ex-smokers say this will go away a few weeks after quitting.

4. Take up exercise if you don't exercise regularly already. It will keep you busy, tire you out, reduce your stress, help you sleep, and distract you.
5. Drink lots of water or juice, and avoid sugared drinks and caffeinated beverages. If weight gain is a concern, seek help from a professional.
6. Set short-term, manageable goals. If your cravings for tobacco are particularly strong, tell yourself, *I'll wait ten minutes; I can hang in there for ten more minutes.* Then when those ten minutes are up, try again. This technique is called "delay." By delaying your gratification for a few moments it is often enough to get you through until the craving passes.
7. Remember, for the former smoker, there is NO SUCH THING AS JUST ONE MORE PUFF or JUST ONE MORE CIGARETTE. Addiction doesn't work that way.
8. Find a trusted friend or two who you can call for support when your cravings are at their worst.
9. Expect to have bad days (when you feel depressed or lethargic) and to experience some downsides to quitting (like mild weight gain). These are normal and

Nicotine Addiction and Your Mind

An insidious part of the addiction is that mental functioning, including concentration, attention, reasoning, and even mathematics performance, gradually becomes dependent on having nicotine present in the brain. A lead nicotine scientist for the National Institute on Drug Abuse, Jack Henningfield, studied these effects for the U.S. armed services, which was concerned about the ability of pilots and other troops in demanding performance situations. His studies found that military performance could become dangerously impaired by the nicotine roller coaster associated with tobacco use. These studies led to actions such as the Navy providing nicotine gum and patches on aircraft carriers, which eventually went smoke-free in the early 1990s.

Within a few hours of smoking, the plummeting nicotine levels leave the brain's mental abilities impaired. Over time, tobacco users need to keep using just to sustain their performance, and the nicotine roller coaster associated with tobacco use keeps them coming back. The good news is that for most people, if they quit smoking, the worst of the mental impairment will be within the first days and planning for it might help. This may mean quitting after exams for example and not right before them. Within a few weeks, as the nicotine withdrawal symptoms decline, mental performance will be as good or better as when on nicotine. For adults, FDA-approved smoking cessation medicines can keep them fully functional. Although they probably work the same way for younger people, there has been less research, so younger people with persisting mental impairment or other withdrawal symptoms should see a health professional who can help decide if a medicine might help.

are NOT failures. But if they get the best of you and you end up blowing it, just dust yourself off and try again. Don't ever quit on quitting.

10. Write down all your reasons for going tobacco-free and keep them in a place where you can remind yourself of them often.

6 Controversial Issues

Despite overwhelming evidence of its dangerous consequences, tobacco promises to remain a threat for years to come. The WHO estimates there are 1.3 billion smokers in the world. Tobacco has enormous *socioeconomic* sway, and in an increasingly global society this means tobacco is already a super power in world affairs.

Tobacco is a unique substance and deserves different attention from other illicit and dangerous drugs. Its place in our society has provoked a great deal of debate. Many people believe smoking should be more government regulated, as other dangerous products are, but others disagree. A typical argument goes something like this:

AGAINST REGULATION: Tobacco is a legal substance and is enjoyed by many people.

FOR REGULATION: Tobacco is the only consumer product that, if used in the intended manner, causes death in a high percentage of its users.

AGAINST REGULATION: But other consumer products have negative health consequences associated with them. Alcohol certainly has health problems associated with its use. Even foods with high fat contents can cause health problems.

FOR REGULATION: The difference is that those other products are not addictive. Tobacco contains nicotine and is addictive. (If you doubt this, just ask anyone who has tried to quit.) Also: potato chips don't cause death when used in their intended manner.

AGAINST REGULATION: But people understand the risks associated with tobacco and freely accept them if they choose to use tobacco.

FOR REGULATION: Certainly adults should be free to make decisions for themselves. However, children should be protected from the advertising and promotion of tobacco products. Since tobacco is addictive and has so many negative health consequences, nontobacco users should not have to pay the health-care costs of tobacco users. The only way to protect children and make tobacco companies pay for health-care costs is to regulate them.

In the end, people who want to use tobacco will do so. With more than one billion smokers in the world, we can expect to interact with smoking for many years to come. Simply outlawing tobacco is not the first step toward a solution. Think of the United States' failed attempt at

Cigarette smoking is a dirty and unattractive habit—but odds are it will continue to be a part of our world.

alcohol prohibition in the early twentieth century. Many people believe outlawing tobacco would produce similar results.

In the past, tobacco companies enjoyed almost completely **uncensored** access to markets, and in some countries, they still do. History has taught us that tobacco companies abuse the freedoms they are given. The trouble is freedom itself: how do the U.S. government and its court systems give tobacco companies and their customers constitutionally secured freedoms—and at the same time protect the freedom of other citizens?

Secondhand Smoke Is Toxic

The EPA classified secondhand smoke as a Class A carcinogen, placing it in the same category as benzene (deadly chemical found in cleaning fluid), asbestos (natural substance closely linked to lung disease), and arsenic (an extremely powerful poison).

Smoking Isn't Just About You:
Secondhand Smoke

Most of the information we have on secondhand smoke comes from a federal agency, the Environmental Protection Agency (EPA). The EPA's first report is called *Respiratory Health Effects of Passive Smoking: Lung Cancer and Other Disorders*, and these are its shocking findings: secondhand cigarette smoking causes 3,000 deaths from lung cancer, 13,000 deaths from other cancers, and 37,000 deaths from lung disease in the United States each year.

The EPA found that secondhand is less toxic than mainstream smoke (inhaled directly by the smoker) but still very dangerous. In fact, the EPA's report claimed that a fifth of all lung cancers resulted from secondhand smoke.

Smoking is no longer just about the smoker. A smoker's freedom—just like any citizen's freedom—ends when others are at risk. Some smokers argue, "Okay, so why don't nonsmokers stay away from smoke?" A nonsmoker might reply to this by pointing out that many nonsmoking individuals encounter situations where they are exposed to cigarette smoke against their will, and that it is unreasonable to expect nonsmokers to avoid all cigarette smoke.

Secondhand smoke is particularly harmful to children because they lack opportunities to escape from secondhand smoke environments. The EPA found much higher rates of lower respiratory tract infections among children living in a smoker's home. They estimated that second-hand smoke causes 150,000 to 300,000 of such infections in children under eighteen months old. The EPA also researched the effect of secondhand smoke on asthma, and found it negative once again. Secondhand smoke significantly complicates asthma among small children. The EPA calculates that secondhand smoke worsens the asthma of 200,000 to one million children each year.

Secondhand smoke also kills newborn children, according to a report published in the March 1995 issue of

Secondhand smoke can be particularly dangerous for women who are pregnant.

Because growing tobacco is an important part of the world's economy, many people are resistant to efforts to reduce the popularity of cigarettes.

the Journal of the American Medical Association. The report was on families in which a child had died from sudden infant death syndrome (SIDS). In SIDS, the infant's heart simply stops beating. SIDS is the leading cause of death among children between the ages of one month and one year. The journal's report stated that infants from homes with more than one smoker were 3.5 times as likely to suffer SIDS.

Tobacco in the Global Economy

We often think of big business growing fat from cigarette smokers' dollars—and while this is one side of the equation, there is another one as well. Farmers around the world, particularly in *third-world nations*, depend on growing tobacco for their livelihood. Simply subtracting this crop from the world economy would have enormous dire effects.

The International Tobacco Growers' Association explains some of the reasons why farmers around the world depend on this crop:

- Tobacco is a legally traded agricultural commodity for which, in global terms, there continues to be brisk demand.
- Tobacco grows on soils with low fertility, subject to leaching of nutrients and erosion. Some tobaccos, such as the Oriental type, are also best grown in arid environments. Such conditions are invariably not suitable for successful production of other crops.
- In many areas where tobacco is grown, crops grown after the cultivation of tobacco benefit from the residual fertilizers in the soil.

- Tobacco growing is a labor-intensive activity that requires vast expertise of farming techniques. The know-how these farmers acquire in tobacco growing frequently proves invaluable in the cultivation of other crops.
- Areas that are distant from air and shipping ports are unsuitable for crops grown in bulk, unless the crop yields high returns that allow for the travel costs to be covered. Tobacco is such a crop; it does not perish or spoil during shipping. Being less perishable than most other potential alternative crops, tobacco can easily be stored.
- There is no more profitable cash crop in most environments suited to tobacco.
- Tobacco enjoys very high price stability.
- As a rule, sale is guaranteed and price negotiated or determined by free auctions.
- Tobacco is, in many areas of the world, the only crop paid for in cash on delivery, or very shortly after.
- In tobacco areas, farms are generally small, requiring high value cash crops to ensure family income.
- Tobacco yields high returns per acre.
- Tobacco-growing attracts sound *infrastructure*, providing financial aid, technical assistance, transport, and storage.
- Successful production of other crops and animal rearing is often more feasible when a high value crop, such as tobacco, is part of the farming system.
- The wealth generated by leaf tobacco production helps to improve quality of life and attracts educational, health, and social facilities in otherwise relatively impoverished, rural areas.

Tobacco is grown all around the world, from Canada to Cuba.

Tobacco—Through the Smoke Screen

Cigarette factories like this one play an enormous role in the world's economy, but ultimately, the decision to smoke or not is a personal one.

Critics of the tobacco industry might say that these are **rationalizations** for a dangerous product. The World Bank has debunked most of these arguments, and the World Health Organization issued a 2005 report showing how tobacco actually contributes to poverty. Be that as it may, the issue is not a simple one; there are no quick and easy answers. Tobacco is a real and ongoing aspect of the world where we all live. Any changes to that fact will be slow and gradual.

You may not feel you have much control over tobacco's place in the world, particularly given the fact that the tobacco industry has millions of dollars' worth of power at its disposal. But here's where you have total control: it's completely up to you whether you choose to smoke.

In the end, only you can make that decision.

Glossary

anxiety disorders: Psychiatric disorders characterized by ongoing feelings of uneasiness and fear when there is no logical cause for such emotions.

biopsies: Removal of tissue samples from a living person for laboratory tests.

chimney sweeps: People who clean chimneys.

colic: Excessive crying in babies caused by stomach and intestinal discomfort.

consensus: General or widespread agreement among all members of a group.

currency: Anything used as money.

dysentery: A disease of the lower intestine, characterized by severe diarrhea, inflammation, and passage of blood and mucus.

emancipating: Freeing.

emphysema: A lung disease in which the air sacs are dilated or enlarged and lack flexibility, leading to impaired breathing.

euphoria: A feeling of great joy, excitement, or well-being.

genetically predisposed: Having the liability to have something because of hereditary makeup.

hernia: A condition in which part of an internal organ projects abnormally through the wall of the cavity that contains it.

hysteria: An emotionally unstable state caused by a traumatic experience.

importation: Bringing into an area.

indigenous: Native to an area.

infrastructure: The large-scale public systems, services, and facilities of a country or region that are necessary for economic activity.

inoperable: Too advanced for effective surgery.

Inquisitors: Officials working for the Inquisition, a medieval organization in the Roman Catholic Church that sought out and punished those who did not hold orthodox religious beliefs.

mass production: The manufacturing of products on a large scale in factories.

mystical: Having supernatural significance.

nephritis: A severe kidney inflammation.

patent: An exclusive right of an inventor to make or sell an invention for a specified period.

rationalizations: Justifications.

rationed: Gave allocated amounts of something to individuals.

small-cell: Small, round or oval cells that resemble grain and contain little cytoplasm.

socioeconomic: Involving social and economic factors.

squamous third-stage B: An advanced form of cancer characterized by flat, scaly cells.

third-world nations: Less developed countries.

thrush: A fungal disease of the mouth, characterized by white patches.

toxic: Poisonous.

transdermal: Introduced through the skin.

uncensored: Without being suppressed.

Further Reading

Dodd, Bill. *1440 Reasons to Quit Smoking: One for Every Minute of the Day*. Minnetonka, Minn.: Meadowbrook, 2000.

Gilman, Sander L., and Xun Zhou. *Smoke: A Global History of Smoking*. New York: Reaktion Books, 2004.

Goodman, Jordan, ed. *Tobacco in History and Culture: An Encyclopedia*. New York: Charles Scribner's Sons, 2004.

Kessler, David. *A Question of Intent*. New York: PublicAffairs, 2001.

Kleinman, Lowell, and Deborah Kleinman. *The Complete Idiot's Guide to Quitting Smoking*. Indianapolis, Ind.: Alpha Books, 2000.

Moe, Barbara. *Teen Smoking and Tobacco Use: A Hot Topic*. Berkeley Heights, N.J.: Enslow, 2000.

Moyer, David B. *The Tobacco Book: A Reference Book of Facts, Figures, and Quotations about Tobacco*. Phoenix, Ariz.: Sunstone Press, 2005.

For More Information

CDC Resources to Quit Smoking
www.cdc.gov/tobacco/how2quit.htm

CDC Surgeon General's Reports
www.cdc.gov/tobacco/data_statistics/sgr/index.htm

CDC Tobacco Control Programs
www.cdc.gov/tobacco/tobacco_control_programs/index.htm

CDC Youth Tobacco Prevention
www.cdc.gov/tobacco/youth/index.htm

Drug Treatment for Nicotine Addiction
Henningfield, Jack E. Reginald V. Fant, August R. Buchhalter, and
Maxine L. Stitzer. "Pharmacotherapy for Nicotine Dependence,"
caonline.amcancersoc.org/cgi/reprint/55/5/281

NIDA Research Report Series: Tobacco/Nicotine
www.drugabuse.gov/drugpages/nicotine.html

WHO and information on International Treaty:
www.who.int/tobacco/framework/download/en/index.html

WHO Water Pipe Report
www.who.int/tobacco/global_interaction/tobreg/
Waterpipe%20recommendation_Final.pdf

World No Tobacco Day Report 2006
www.who.int/tobacco/communications/events/wntd/2006/
Tfi_Rapport.pdf

The websites listed on this page were active at the time of publication. The publisher is not responsible for websites that have changed their addresses or discontinued operation since the date of publication. The publisher will review and update the website list upon each reprint.

Bibliography

American Heart Association. "Tobacco Industry's Targeting of Youth, Minorities, and Women." http://www.americanheart.org/presenter.jhtml?identifier=11226.

Amos, Amanda. "Creating a Global Tobacco Culture Among Women." Smoke Free Europe. http://www.health.fi/smoke2html/Pages/Smoke2-23.html.

"Anti-Tobacco Campaigns in Native American Communities." PBS. http://www.pbs.org/ttc/health/natamtobacco.html.

Borio, Gene. "Tobacco Timeline." 2006 Tobacco Org. June 2006. http://www.tobacco.org/History/Tobacco_History.html.

"Brief History of Tobacco." 2001 Syndistar. http://www.intheknow-zone.com/tobacco/history.htm.

Brown, Virginia, ed. *Southern Indian Myths and Legends*. Birmingham, Ala.: Beechwood Books, 1985.

Centers for Disease Control and Prevention. "Cigarette Smoking Among Adults—United States 2002." May 28, 2004. http://www.cdc.gov/mmwr/preview/mmwrhtml/mm5320a2.htm.

Centers for Disease Control and Prevention. "Cigarette Smoking-Related Mortality." 2001. http://www.cdc.gov/TOBACCO/research_data/health_consequences/mortali.htm.

Centers for Disease Control and Prevention. "Targeting Tobacco Use: The Nation's Leading Cause of Death." 2006. http://www.cdc.gov/nccdphp/publications/aag/osh.htm.

Hyde, Margaret, and John Setaro. *Smoking 101*. Minneapolis, Minn.: Twenty-First Century Books, 2006.

Kessler, David. A *Question of Intent*. New York: Public Affairs, 2001.

Kluger, Richard. *Ashes to Ashes*. New York: Alfred A. Knopf, 1996.

"Minority Cigarette Marketing Scrutinized." The Associated

Press, August 8, 2004. http://www.11alive.com/news/news_article. aspx?storyid=50686.

"The Science Behind Tobacco." Liberty Science Center. http://www.lsc.org/tobacco/farming/plant.html.

"Selling Tobacco." Media Awareness Network. http://www.media-awareness.ca/english/resources/educational/lessons/elementary/to-bacco/selling_tobacco.cfm.

"Should Tobacco Be Legal?" Conscientious Consuming. http://www.consuming.com/Tobacco/should_tobacco_be_legal.htm.

Pietrusza, David. *Smoking*. San Diego, Calif.: Lucent Books, 1997.

"Tobacco Policy." *News Batch*. http://www.newsbatch.com/tobacco.htm.

"Women and Smoking." CDC Surgeon General's Report. http://www.cdc.gov/tobacco/sgr/sgr_forwomen/factsheet_marketing.htm.

Index

Picture Credits

Atkins, Mark–Fotolia: p. 86
Boojoo–Fotolia: p. 52
Cairon, Jose Vicente–Fotolia: p. 75
Dietrick, Marc–Fotolia: p. 62
Dimitri Designer: p. 93
Gavric, Mitar–Fotolia: p. 10
Gehant, Laurent–Fotolia: p. 76
iStockphotos: p. 82
    Brizendine, Jonathan: p. 73
    Cervo, Diego: p. 96
    Knape, Satu: p. 80
    Littleq, Maryann: p. 115
    Millanovic: p. 116
    Niezabitowski, Jakub: p. 112
    Rodgers, Loren: p. 71
    Sanchez, Roberto A.: p. 8
Kaulitzki, Sebastian–Fotolia: p. 66
Kornilov, Oleg–Fotolia: p. 106
Mazur, Bogoslaus–Fotolia: p. 84
Miller, Katrina–Fotolia: p. 88
Ostojic, Branislav–Fotolia: p. 40
Pityves–Fotolia: p. 79
Sirokin, Nikolai–Fotolia: p. 98
Smitea–Fotolia: p. 56
Snider, Lee: p. 54
Tadija–Fotolia: pp. 36
Tymszan, Lucaza–Fotolia: p. 109
University of Montana: p. 21
U.S. National Library of Medicine: p. 35
Weitzel, Thomas–Fotolia: p. 28
Yurlov, Andrey–Fotolia: p. 60
Zdorov, Kirill–Fotolia: p. 111

To the best knowledge of the publisher, all other images are in the public domain. If any image has been inadvertently uncredited, please notify Harding House Publishing Services, Vestal, New York 13850, so that rectification can be made for future printings.

Author and Consultant Biographies

Author

Zachary Chastain is a writer and actor living in Binghamton, New York. He has written many educational books for students of all ages on health, history, and the arts.

Series Consultant

Jack E. Henningfield, Ph.D., is a professor at the Johns Hopkins University School of Medicine, and he is also Vice President for Research and Health Policy at Pinney Associates, a consulting firm in Bethesda, Maryland, that specializes in science policy and regulatory issues concerning public health, medications development, and behavior-focused disease management. Dr. Henningfield has contributed information relating to addiction to numerous reports of the U.S. Surgeon General, the National Academy of Sciences, and the World Health Organization.